Cram101 Textbook Outlines to accompany:

Law and Economics

Robert D. Cooter, 5th Edition

A Cram101 Inc. publication (c) 2010.

Cram101 Textbook Outlines and Cram101.com are Cram101 Inc. publications and services. All notes, highlights, reviews, and practice tests are written and prepared by Cram101, all rights reserved.

PRACTICE EXAMS.

Get all of the self-teaching practice exams for each chapter of this textbook at **www.Cram101.com** and ace the tests. Here is an example:

Chapter 1

Law and Economics
Robert D. Cooter, 5th Edition,
All Material Written and Prepared by Cram101

I WANT A BETTER GRADE.   Items 1 - 50 of 100.

1. _____ is an economic model based on price, utility and quantity in a market. It concludes that in a competitive market, price will function to equalize the quantity demanded by consumers, and the quantity supplied by producers, resulting in an economic equilibrium of price and quantity.

    The demand schedule, depicted graphically as the demand curve, represents the amount of goods that buyers are willing and able to purchase at various prices, assuming all other non-price factors remain the same.

    - Supply and demand
    - S corporation
    - S corporations
    - S&P GSCI

2. In economics, _____ refers to the primarily social and political value of an anecdote or anecdotal evidence in promoting understanding of a social, cultural, in the last several decades the evaluation of anecdotes has received sustained academic scrutiny from economists and scholars such as S.G. Checkland (on David Ricardo), Steven Novella, Hollis Robbins, R. Charleton, Kwamena Kwansah-Aidoo, and others; these academics seek to quantify the value inherent in the deployment of anecdotes. More recently, economists studying choice models have begun assessing _____ in the context of framing; Kahneman and Tversky suggest that choice models may be contingent on stories or anecdotes that frame or influence choice.

    - Anecdotal value
    - Abacus
    - Abandonment
    - Abbott Payson Usher

3. _____ are a form of damages available as a recourse to a breached contract. When a contracting party fails to fulfill their contractual duties, which causes losses to the other party, the party in breach can be liable for the

---

You get a 50% discount for the online exams. Go to **Cram101.com**, click Sign Up at the top of the screen, and enter DK73DW8473 in the promo code box on the registration screen. Access to Cram101.com is $4.95 per month, cancel at any time.

With Cram101.com online, you also have access to extensive reference material.

You will nail those essays and papers. Here is an example from a Cram101 Biology text:

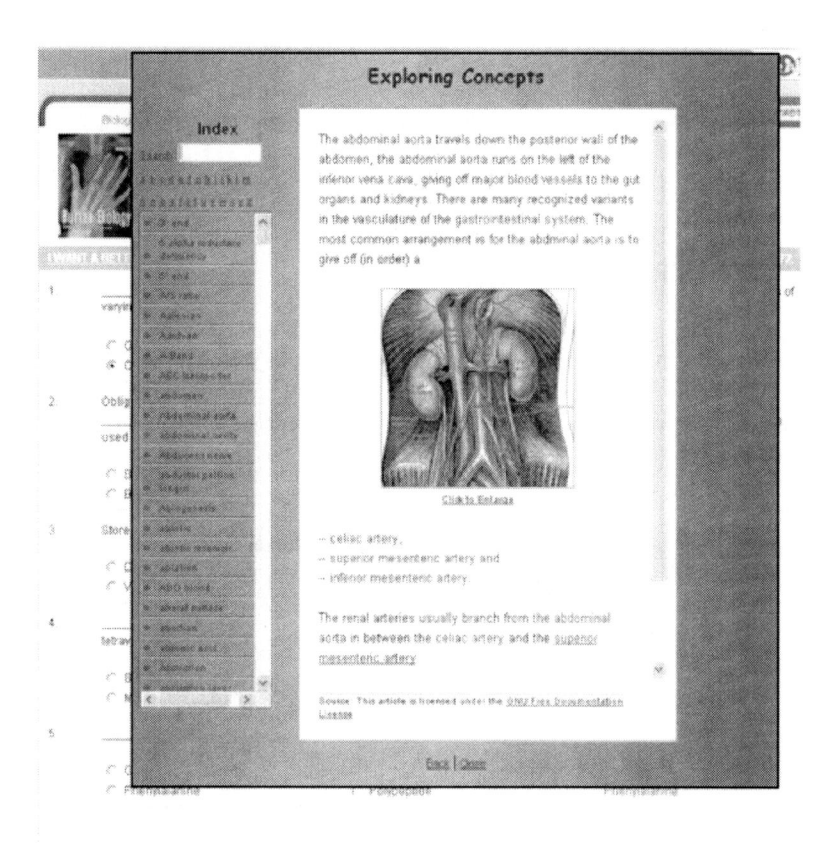

Visit **www.Cram101.com**, click Sign Up at the top of the screen, and enter DK73DW8473 in the promo code box on the registration screen. Access to www.Cram101.com is normally $9.95 per month, but because you have purchased this book, your access fee is only $4.95 per month, cancel at any time. Sign up and stop highlighting textbooks forever.

Learning System

Cram101 Textbook Outlines is a learning system. The notes in this book are the highlights of your textbook, you will never have to highlight a book again.

How to use this book. Take this book to class, it is your notebook for the lecture. The notes and highlights on the left hand side of the pages follow the outline and order of the textbook. All you have to do is follow along while your instructor presents the lecture. Circle the items emphasized in class and add other important information on the right side. With Cram101 Textbook Outlines you'll spend less time writing and more time listening. Learning becomes more efficient.

Cram101.com Online

Increase your studying efficiency by using Cram101.com's practice tests and online reference material. It is the perfect complement to Cram101 Textbook Outlines. Use self-teaching matching tests or simulate in-class testing with comprehensive multiple choice tests, or simply use Cram's true and false tests for quick review. Cram101.com even allows you to enter your in-class notes for an integrated studying format combining the textbook notes with your class notes.

Visit **www.Cram101.com**, click Sign Up at the top of the screen, and enter **DK73DW8473** in the promo code box on the registration screen. Access to www.Cram101.com is normally $9.95 per month, but because you have purchased this book, your access fee is only $4.95 per month. Sign up and stop highlighting textbooks forever.

Copyright © 2010 by Cram101, Inc. All rights reserved. "Cram101"® and "Never Highlight a Book Again!"® are registered trademarks of Cram101, Inc. ISBN(s): 9781428849884. EDE-1.2009128

Law and Economics
Robert D. Cooter, 5th

CONTENTS

1. AN INTRODUCTION TO LAW AND ECONOMICS 2
2. A REVIEW OF MICROECONOMIC THEORY 12
3. AN INTRODUCTION TO LAW AND LEGAL INSTITUTIONS 42
4. AN ECONOMIC THEORY OF PROPERTY 50
5. TOPICS IN THE ECONOMICS OF PROPERTY LAW 66
6. AN ECONOMIC THEORY OF CONTRACT 94
7. TOPICS IN THE ECONOMICS OF CONTRACT LAW 110
8. AN ECONOMIC THEORY OF TORT LAW 128
9. TOPICS IN THE ECONOMICS OF TORT LIABILITY 138
10. AN ECONOMIC THEORY OF THE LEGAL PROCESS 154
11. AN ECONOMIC THEORY OF CRIME AND PUNISHMENT 172
12. TOPICS IN THE ECONOMICS OF CRIME AND PUNISHMENT 180

Chapter 1. AN INTRODUCTION TO LAW AND ECONOMICS

Supply and demand	Supply and demand is an economic model based on price, utility and quantity in a market. It concludes that in a competitive market, price will function to equalize the quantity demanded by consumers, and the quantity supplied by producers, resulting in an economic equilibrium of price and quantity. The demand schedule, depicted graphically as the demand curve, represents the amount of goods that buyers are willing and able to purchase at various prices, assuming all other non-price factors remain the same.
Anecdotal value	In economics, Anecdotal value refers to the primarily social and political value of an anecdote or anecdotal evidence in promoting understanding of a social, cultural, in the last several decades the evaluation of anecdotes has received sustained academic scrutiny from economists and scholars such as S.G. Checkland (on David Ricardo), Steven Novella, Hollis Robbins, R. Charleton, Kwamena Kwansah-Aidoo, and others; these academics seek to quantify the value inherent in the deployment of anecdotes. More recently, economists studying choice models have begun assessing Anecdotal value in the context of framing; Kahneman and Tversky suggest that choice models may be contingent on stories or anecdotes that frame or influence choice.
Expectation damages	Expectation damages are a form of damages available as a recourse to a breached contract. When a contracting party fails to fulfill their contractual duties, which causes losses to the other party, the party in breach can be liable for the losses of the other party. Losses that relate to the consequences of breach are Expectation damages, because the purpose of this type of remedy is to put the plaintiff in the position he would have been in had the contract been fulfilled.
Elawyering	The term Elawyering or e-lawyering is a neologism used to refer to the practice of law over the Internet, in a way more expansive than a mere legal related internet advertisement for a service, lawyer, Elawyering initiatives have been undertaken by the American Bar Association in order to reach a "latent market" of lower and middle class citizens in need of legal services. Lawyers practicing law online are also referred to as "virtual lawyers" and practice from virtual law offices.
Regulation	Regulation refers to "controlling human or societal behaviour by rules or restrictions." Regulation can take many forms: legal restrictions promulgated by a government authority, self-Regulation, social Regulation (e.g. norms), co-Regulation and market Regulation. One can consider Regulation as actions of conduct imposing sanctions (such as a fine). This action of administrative law, or implementing regulatory law, may be contrasted with statutory or case law.
Tort	Tort law is a body of law that addresses, and provides remedies for, civil wrongs not arising out of contractual obligations. A person who suffers legal damages may be able to use Tort law to receive compensation from someone who is legally responsible, or liable, for those injuries. Generally speaking, Tort law defines what constitutes a legal injury and establishes the circumstances under which one person may be held liable for another"s injury.
Deregulation	Deregulation is the removal or simplification of government rules and regulations that constrain the operation of market forces. Deregulation does not mean elimination of laws against fraud, but eliminating or reducing government control of how business is done, thereby moving toward a more free market.

Chapter 1. AN INTRODUCTION TO LAW AND ECONOMICS

Chapter 1. AN INTRODUCTION TO LAW AND ECONOMICS

	The stated rationale f is often that fewer and simpler regulations will lead to a raised level of competitiveness, therefore higher productivity, more efficiency and lower prices overall.
Markets	A market is any one of a variety of different systems, institutions, procedures, social relations and infrastructures whereby persons trade, and goods and services are exchanged, forming part of the economy. It is an arrangement that allows buyers and sellers to exchange things. markets vary in size, range, geographic scale, location, types and variety of human communities, as well as the types of goods and services traded.
Market Equilibrium	In economics, economic equilibrium is simply a state of the world where economic forces are balanced and in the absence of external influences the (equilibrium) values of economic variables will not change. It is the point at which quantity demanded and quantity supplied are equal. Market equilibrium, for example, refers to a condition where a market price is established through competition such that the amount of goods or services sought by buyers is equal to the amount of goods or services produced by sellers.
Macro derivative	A macro derivative or an economic derivative is a derivative that is based on a macroeconomic figure, such as consumer confidence, jobless claims, in 2002 Goldman Sachs and Deutsche Bank announced to offer their clients auctions for derivatives based on macroeconomic key figures. In 2005 Deutsche Bank left the joint project.
Coase Theorem	In law and economics, the Coase theorem, attributed to Ronald Coase, describes the economic efficiency of an economic allocation or outcome in the presence of externalities. The theorem states that when trade in an externality is possible and there are no transaction costs, bargaining will lead to an efficient outcome regardless of the initial allocation of property rights. In practice, obstacles to bargaining or poorly defined property rights can prevent Coasian bargaining.
Hindsight bias	Hindsight bias is the inclination to see events that have occurred as more predictable than they in fact were before they took place. hindsight bias has been demonstrated experimentally in a variety of settings, including politics, games and medicine. In psychological experiments of hindsight bias, subjects also tend to remember their predictions of future events as having been stronger than they actually were, in those cases where those predictions turn out correct.
Pareto efficiency	Pareto efficiency, is an important concept in economics with broad applications in game theory, engineering and the social sciences. The term is named after Vilfredo Pareto, an Italian economist who used the concept in his studies of economic efficiency and income distribution. Informally, Pareto efficient situations are those in which any change to make any person better off is impossible without making someone else worse off.
Preference	Preference is a concept, used in the social sciences, particularly economics. It assumes a real or imagined "choice" between alternatives and the possibility of rank ordering of these alternatives, based on happiness, satisfaction, gratification, enjoyment, utility they provide. More generally, it can be seen as a source of motivation.

Chapter 1. AN INTRODUCTION TO LAW AND ECONOMICS

Chapter 1. AN INTRODUCTION TO LAW AND ECONOMICS

Price	Price in economics and business is the result of an exchange and from that trade we assign a numerical monetary value to a good, service or asset. If Alice trades Bob 4 apples for an orange, the price of an orange is 4 apples. Inversely, the price of an apple is 1/4 oranges.
Dot-com bubble	The "Dot-com bubble" (or) was a speculative bubble covering roughly 1998-2001 (with a climax on March 10, 2000 with the NASDAQ peaking at 5132.52) during which stock markets in Western nations saw their equity value rise rapidly from growth in the more recent Internet sector and related fields. While the latter part was a boom and bust cycle, the Internet boom sometimes is meant to refer to the steady commercial growth of the Internet with the advent of the world wide web as exemplified by the first release of the Mosaic web browser in 1993 and continuing through the 1990s. The period was marked by the founding (and, in many cases, spectacular failure) of a group of new Internet-based companies commonly referred to as dot-coms.
Social	The term social refers to a characteristic of living organisms (humans in particular, though biologists also apply the term to populations of other animals). It always refers to the interaction of organisms with other organisms and to their collective co-existence, irrespective of whether they are aware of it or not, and irrespective of whether the interaction is voluntary or involuntary. In the absence of agreement about its meaning, the term "ps" is used in many different senses and regarded as a [[]], referringse among other things to: · Attitudes, orientations, or behaviours which take the interests, intentions, or needs of other people into account (in contrast to anti-social behaviour);has played some role in defining the idea or the principle. For instance terms like social realism, social justice, social constructivism, social psychology and social capital imply that there is some social process involved or considered, a process that is not there in regular, "non-social", realism, justice, constructivism, psychology, or capital.
Distribution	Distribution in economics refers to the way total output or income is distributed among individuals or among the factors of production (labor, land, and capital) (Samuelson and Nordhaus, 2001, p. 762). In general theory and the national income and product accounts, each unit of output corresponds to a unit of income. One use of national accounts is for classifying factor incomes and measuring their respective shares, as in National Income.
Damages	In law, Damages are money claimed by or ordered to be paid to a person as compensation for loss or injury. Compensatory Damages, also called actual Damages, are paid to compensate the claimant for loss, injury, or harm suffered by another"s breach of duty. On a breach of contract by a defendant, a court generally awards the sum that would restore the injured party to the economic position they expected from performance of the promise or promises (known as an "expectation measure" or "benefit-of-the-bargain" measure of Damages).
Economic efficiency	Economic efficiency is used to refer to a number of related concepts. It is the using of resources in such a way as to maximize the production of goods and services. A system can be called economically efficient if:

Chapter 1. AN INTRODUCTION TO LAW AND ECONOMICS

Chapter 1. AN INTRODUCTION TO LAW AND ECONOMICS

	· No one can be made better off without making someone else worse off. · More output cannot be obtained without increasing the amount of inputs. · Production proceeds at the lowest possible per-unit cost. These definitions of efficiency are not equivalent, but they are all encompassed by the idea that nothing more can be achieved given the resources available.
Income redistribution	In economics, redistribution is the transfer of income, wealth or property from some individuals to others. income redistribution evens the amount of income that individuals are permitted to earn, in order to correct the ineffectiveness of a market economy to remunerate based on the amount of labor expended by an individual. The objective of moderate income redistribution is to avoid the unjust equalization of incomes on one side and unjust extremes of concentration on the other sides.
Cost	In business, retail, and accounting, a cost is the value of money that has been used up to produce something, and hence is not available for use anymore. In economics, a cost is an alternative that is given up as a result of a decision. In business, the cost may be one of acquisition, in which case the amount of money expended to acquire it is counted as cost.
Transaction cost	In economics and related disciplines, a Transaction cost is a cost incurred in making an economic exchange (restated: the cost of participating in a market). For example, most people, when buying or selling a stock, must pay a commission to their broker; that commission is a Transaction cost of doing the stock deal. Or consider buying a banana from a store; to purchase the banana, your costs will be not only the price of the banana itself, but also the energy and effort it requires to find out which of the various banana products you prefer, where to get them and at what price, the cost of traveling from your house to the store and back, the time waiting in line, and the effort of the paying itself; the costs above and beyond the cost of the banana are the Transaction costs.
Tax	To Tax is to impose a financial charge or other levy upon a Taxpayer (an individual or legal entity) by a state or the functional equivalent of a state such that failure to pay is punishable by law. Taxes are also imposed by many subnational entities. Taxes consist of direct Tax or indirect Tax, and may be paid in money or as its labour equivalent (often but not always unpaid).
Amendment	A constitutional amendment is a change to the constitution of a nation or a state. In jurisdictions with "rigid" or "entrenched" constitutions, amendments require a special procedure different from that used for enacting ordinary laws. · 1 Referendum

Chapter 1. AN INTRODUCTION TO LAW AND ECONOMICS

Chapter 1. AN INTRODUCTION TO LAW AND ECONOMICS

- 1.1 Successive majorities
- 1.2 Special requirements in federations
- 1.3 Mixed systems
- 2

Some jurisdictions require that an amendment be approved by the legislature on two separate occasions during two separate but consecutive terms, with a general election in the interim. Under some of these constitutions there must be a dissolution of the legislature and an immediate general election on the occasion that an amendment is adopted for the first time.

Chapter 1. AN INTRODUCTION TO LAW AND ECONOMICS

Chapter 2. A REVIEW OF MICROECONOMIC THEORY

Elawyering	The term Elawyering or e-lawyering is a neologism used to refer to the practice of law over the Internet, in a way more expansive than a mere legal related internet advertisement for a service, lawyer, Elawyering initiatives have been undertaken by the American Bar Association in order to reach a "latent market" of lower and middle class citizens in need of legal services. Lawyers practicing law online are also referred to as "virtual lawyers" and practice from virtual law offices.
Regulation	Regulation refers to "controlling human or societal behaviour by rules or restrictions." Regulation can take many forms: legal restrictions promulgated by a government authority, self-Regulation, social Regulation (e.g. norms), co-Regulation and market Regulation. One can consider Regulation as actions of conduct imposing sanctions (such as a fine). This action of administrative law, or implementing regulatory law, may be contrasted with statutory or case law.
Tort	Tort law is a body of law that addresses, and provides remedies for, civil wrongs not arising out of contractual obligations. A person who suffers legal damages may be able to use Tort law to receive compensation from someone who is legally responsible, or liable, for those injuries. Generally speaking, Tort law defines what constitutes a legal injury and establishes the circumstances under which one person may be held liable for another"s injury.
Anecdotal value	In economics, Anecdotal value refers to the primarily social and political value of an anecdote or anecdotal evidence in promoting understanding of a social, cultural, in the last several decades the evaluation of anecdotes has received sustained academic scrutiny from economists and scholars such as S.G. Checkland (on David Ricardo), Steven Novella, Hollis Robbins, R. Charleton, Kwamena Kwansah-Aidoo, and others; these academics seek to quantify the value inherent in the deployment of anecdotes. More recently, economists studying choice models have begun assessing Anecdotal value in the context of framing; Kahneman and Tversky suggest that choice models may be contingent on stories or anecdotes that frame or influence choice.
Consumer	Consumer is a broad label that refers to any individuals or households that use goods and services generated within the economy. The concept of a Consumer is used in different contexts, so that the usage and significance of the term may vary. Typically when business people and economists talk of Consumers they are talking about person as Consumer, an aggregated commodity item with little individuality other than that expressed in the buy/not-buy decision.
Natural monopoly	In economics, a Natural monopoly occurs when, due to the economies of scale of a particular industry, the maximum efficiency of production and distribution is realized through a single supplier. Natural monopolies arise where the largest supplier in an industry, often the first supplier in a market, has an overwhelming cost advantage over other actual or potential competitors. This tends to be the case in industries where capital costs predominate, creating economies of scale which are large in relation to the size of the market, and hence high barriers to entry; examples include water services and electricity.
Choice	There are four types of decisions, although they can be expressed in different ways. Brian Tracy, who often uses enumerated lists in his talks, breaks them down into:

Chapter 2. A REVIEW OF MICROECONOMIC THEORY

Chapter 2. A REVIEW OF MICROECONOMIC THEORY

- Command decisions, which can only be made by you, as the "Commander in Chief"; or owner of a company.
- Delegated decisions, which may be made by anyone, such as the color of the bike shed, and should be delegated, as the decision must be made but the Choice is inconsequential.
- Avoided decisions, where the outcome could be so severe that the Choice should not be made, as the consequences can not be recovered from if the wrong Choice is made. This will most likely result in negative actions, such as death.
- "No-brainer" decisions, where the Choice is so obvious that only one Choice can reasonably be made.

A fifth type, however, or fourth if three and four are combined as one type, is the collaborative decision, which should be made in consultation with, and by agreement of others.

Self-sufficiency

Self-sufficiency refers to the state of not requiring any outside aid, support, for survival; it is therefore a type of personal or collective autonomy. On a large scale, a totally self-sufficient economy that does not trade with the outside world is called an autarky.

The term Self-sufficiency is usually applied to varieties of sustainable living in which nothing is consumed outside of what is produced by the self-sufficient individuals.

Possession

The word Possession might refer to:

- Possession (1981 film), starring Sam Neill, Isabelle Adjani; dir. by Andrzej Zulawski
- Possession (2002 film), adaptation of the A. S. Byatt novel; with Aaron Eckhart and Gwyneth Paltrow
- Possession (2009 film), starring Sarah Michelle Gellar and Lee Pace
- Possession (TV series), 1985 Australian series
- Possession (video game), a possibly cancelled console game
- Possession (Iron Butterfly song), song by American psychedelic rock band Iron Butterfly
- Possession , a 1989 song and one of the singles taken from Bad English"s self-titled debut album
- Possession , a 1993 song by Sarah McLachlan on her album Fumbling Towards Ecstasy
- "Possession", song on the 2005 Mandaryna.com2me album by the Polish singer Mandaryna
- "Possession", a song by death metal band Whitechapel

- La Possession, French commune on the Indian Ocean island of Réunion
- Possession Point, former land form, Hong Kong
- Possession Sound, Washington state
- Possession Street, Hong Kong

- Dependent territory, an area of land over which another country exercises sovereignty, but which does not have the full right of participation in that country"s governance
- Ownership
- Possession (law), exclusive practical control of a thing, in the context of the legal implications of that control
- Title (property)
- Drug Possession, a crime

Chapter 2. A REVIEW OF MICROECONOMIC THEORY

Chapter 2. A REVIEW OF MICROECONOMIC THEORY

· Inalienable Possession, relationship between two objects that is irreversible
· Possession (linguistics), grammatically expressed relationship such as control-of and ownership-of

· Possession (novel), 1990 novel by A. S. Byatt

· Demonic Possession, belief in the control of a person by the Devil or other malevolent spirit
· Spirit Possession, belief in the control of the behavior of a living thing or natural object by a spiritual being .

Maximization	Maximization is an economics theory, that refers to individuals or societies gaining the maximum amount out of the resources they have available to them. The theory proposed by most economists is that Maximization refers to the Maximization of profit. As some economists have begun to find out, this theory does not hold true for all people and cultures. The profit motive is not universal, and the profit motive does not seem to be applicable in all cases. Furthermore, Maximization does not ensure optimization; i.e. the maximum level of resource use is not necessarily the optimal level.
Utility	In economics, Utility is a measure of the relative satisfaction from or desirability of, consumption of various goods and services. Given this measure, one may speak meaningfully of increasing or decreasing Utility, and thereby explain economic behavior in terms of attempts to increase one"s Utility. For illustrative purposes, changes in Utility are sometimes expressed in fictional units called utils (fictional in that there is no standard scale for them).
Allocative efficiency	Allocative efficiency is a theoretical measure of the benefit or utility derived from a proposed or actual choice in the distribution or apportionment of resources. Although there are different standards of evaluation for the concept of Allocative efficiency, the basic principle asserts that in any economic system, choices in resource allocation produce both "winners" and "losers" relative to the choice being evaluated. The principles of rational choice, individual maximization, utilitarianism and market theory further suppose that the outcomes for winners and losers can be identified, compared and measured.
Coase Theorem	In law and economics, the Coase theorem, attributed to Ronald Coase, describes the economic efficiency of an economic allocation or outcome in the presence of externalities. The theorem states that when trade in an externality is possible and there are no transaction costs, bargaining will lead to an efficient outcome regardless of the initial allocation of property rights. In practice, obstacles to bargaining or poorly defined property rights can prevent Coasian bargaining.
Comparative statics	In economics, Comparative statics is the comparison of two different economic outcomes, before and after a change in some underlying exogenous parameter (Mas-Colell, Whinston, and Green, 1995, p. 24). As a study of statics it compares two different equilibrium states, after the process of adjustment (if any). It does not study the motion towards equilibrium, nor the process of the change itself.

Chapter 2. A REVIEW OF MICROECONOMIC THEORY

Chapter 2. A REVIEW OF MICROECONOMIC THEORY

Pareto efficiency	Pareto efficiency, is an important concept in economics with broad applications in game theory, engineering and the social sciences. The term is named after Vilfredo Pareto, an Italian economist who used the concept in his studies of economic efficiency and income distribution. Informally, Pareto efficient situations are those in which any change to make any person better off is impossible without making someone else worse off.
Dependent variable	The terms "Dependent variable" and "inDependent variable" are used in similar but subtly different ways in mathematics and statistics as part of the standard terminology in those subjects. They are used to distinguish between two types of quantities being considered, separating them into those available at the start of a process and those being created by it, where the latter (Dependent variables) are dependent on the former (inDependent variables). The inDependent variable is typically the variable being manipulated or changed and the Dependent variable is the observed result of the inDependent variable being manipulated.
Independent variable	The terms "dependent variable" and "Independent variable" are used in similar but subtly different ways in mathematics and statistics as part of the standard terminology in those subjects. They are used to distinguish between two types of quantities being considered, separating them into those available at the start of a process and those being created by it, where the latter (dependent variables) are dependent on the former (Independent variables). The Independent variable is typically the variable being manipulated or changed and the dependent variable is the observed result of the Independent variable being manipulated.
Direct relationship	In mathematics and statistics, a positive is a relationship between two variables in which change in one variable is associated with a change in the other variable in the same direction. For example all linear relationships with a positive slope are Direct relationships. In a Direct relationship, as one variable, say x, increases, the other variable, say y, also increases, and if one variable decreases, the other variable decreases.
Slope	In mathematics, the Slope or gradient of a line describes its steepness, incline, or grade. A higher Slope value indicates a steeper incline. The Slope is defined as the ratio of the "rise" divided by the "run" between two points on a line, or in other words, the ratio of the altitude change to the horizontal distance between any two points on the line.
Inverse relationship	An Inverse relationship or negative relationship is a mathematical relationship in which one variable, say y, decreases as another, say x, increases. For a linear (straight-line) relation, this can be expressed as $y = a - bx$, where -b is a constant value less than zero and a is a constant. For example, there is an Inverse relationship between education and unemployment -- that is, as education increases, the rate of unemployment decreases.

Chapter 2. A REVIEW OF MICROECONOMIC THEORY

Chapter 2. A REVIEW OF MICROECONOMIC THEORY

Nonlinear	In mathematics, a nonlinear system is a system which is not linear, that is, a system which does not satisfy the superposition principle, a nonlinear system is any problem where the variable(s) to be solved for cannot be written as a linear combination of independent components. A nonhomogeneous system, which is linear apart from the presence of a function of the independent variables, is nonlinear according to a strict definition, but such systems are usually studied alongside linear systems, because they can be transformed to a linear system of multiple variables.
Demand	In economics, demand is the desire to own anything and the ability to pay for it. . The term demand signifies the ability or the willingness to buy a particular commodity at a given point of time.
Preference	Preference is a concept, used in the social sciences, particularly economics. It assumes a real or imagined "choice" between alternatives and the possibility of rank ordering of these alternatives, based on happiness, satisfaction, gratification, enjoyment, utility they provide. More generally, it can be seen as a source of motivation.
Budget	Budget generally refers to a list of all planned expenses and revenues. It is a plan for saving and spending. A Budget is an important concept in microeconomics, which uses a Budget line to illustrate the trade-offs between two or more goods.
Indifference curve	In microeconomic theory, an Indifference curve is a graph showing different bundles of goods, each measured as to quantity, between which a consumer is indifferent. That is, at each point on the curve, the consumer has no preference for one bundle over another. In other words, they are all equally preferred.
Preference map	In microeconomic theory a Preference map or indifference map is the collection of indifference curves possessed by an individual. Similar in nature to a topographical map, the contour lines of such a map demonstrating progressively more desirable options as they move upward or to the right. Because of the nature of indifference curves they cannot intersect and are effectively infinite in number, their sum defining all possible combinations of values.
Damages	In law, Damages are money claimed by or ordered to be paid to a person as compensation for loss or injury. Compensatory Damages, also called actual Damages, are paid to compensate the claimant for loss, injury, or harm suffered by another"s breach of duty. On a breach of contract by a defendant, a court generally awards the sum that would restore the injured party to the economic position they expected from performance of the promise or promises (known as an "expectation measure" or "benefit-of-the-bargain" measure of Damages).
Marginal cost	In economics and finance, Marginal cost is the change in total cost that arises when the quantity produced changes by one unit. It is the cost of producing one more unit of a good. Mathematically, the Marginal cost function is expressed as the first derivative of the total cost (TC) function with respect to quantity (Q).

Chapter 2. A REVIEW OF MICROECONOMIC THEORY

Chapter 2. A REVIEW OF MICROECONOMIC THEORY

Price-specie-flow mechanism	The price-specie-flow mechanism is a logical argument by David Hume against the Mercantilist (1700-1776) idea that a nation should strive for a positive balance of trade, a system in which gold is the official means of international payments and each nation"s currency is in the form of gold itself or of paper currency fully convertible into gold. Hume argued that when a country with a gold standard had a positive balance of trade, gold would flow into the country in the amount that the value of exports exceeds the value of imports.
Demand curve	In economics, the Demand curve can be defined as the graph depicting the relationship between the price of a certain commodity, and the amount of it that consumers are willing and able to purchase at that given price. It is a graphic representation of a demand schedule. The Demand curve for all consumers together follows from the Demand curve of every individual consumer: the individual demands at each price are added together.
Ceteris paribus	CÄ"terÄ«s paribus is a Latin phrase, literally translated as "with other things the same," or "all other things being equal or held constant." It is commonly rendered in English as "all other things being equal." A prediction, or a statement about causal or logical connections between two states of affairs, is qualified by Ceteris paribus in order to acknowledge, and to rule out, the possibility of other factors that could override the relationship between the antecedent and the consequent. A Ceteris paribus assumption is often fundamental to the predictive purpose of scientific inquiry. In order to formulate scientific laws, it is usually necessary to rule out factors which interfere with examining a specific causal relationship.
Elasticity	In economics, elasticity is the ratio of the percent change in one variable to the percent change in another variable. It is a tool for measuring the responsiveness of a function to changes in parameters in a relative way. Commonly analyzed are elasticity of substitution, price and wealth.
Price elasticity of demand	Price elasticity of demand (PED) is defined as the measure of responsiveness in the quantity demanded for a commodity as a result of change in price of the same commodity. It is a measure of how consumers react to a change in price. In other words, it is percentage change in quantity demanded by the percentage change in price of the same commodity.
Price	Price in economics and business is the result of an exchange and from that trade we assign a numerical monetary value to a good, service or asset. If Alice trades Bob 4 apples for an orange, the price of an orange is 4 apples. Inversely, the price of an apple is 1/4 oranges.
The demand	Perfectly inelastic demand Perfectly elastic demand A price fall usually results in an increase in the quantity demanded by consumers . The demand for a good is relatively inelastic when the change in quantity demanded is less than change in price. Goods and services for which no substitutes exist are generally inelastic.

Chapter 2. A REVIEW OF MICROECONOMIC THEORY

Chapter 2. A REVIEW OF MICROECONOMIC THEORY

Monopoly	In economics, a Monopoly exists when a specific individual or an enterprise has sufficient control over a particular product or service to determine significantly the terms on which other individuals shall have access to it. Monopolies are thus characterized by a lack of economic competition for the good or service that they provide and a lack of viable substitute goods. The verb "monopolize" refers to the process by which a firm gains persistently greater market share than what is expected under perfect competition.
Total cost	In economics, and cost accounting, Total cost describes the total economic cost of production and is made up of variable costs, which vary according to the quantity of a good produced and include inputs such as labor and raw materials, plus fixed costs, which are independent of the quantity of a good produced and include inputs (capital) that cannot be varied in the short term, such as buildings and machinery. Total cost in economics includes the total opportunity cost of each factor of production in addition to fixed and variable costs. The rate at which Total cost changes as the amount produced changes is called marginal cost.
Total revenue	Total revenue is the total money received from the sale of any given quantity of output. The total revenue is calculated by taking the price of the sale times the quantity sold, i.e. total revenue = price X quantity.
Contract	In common-law systems, the five key requirements for the creation of a contract are: 1. offer and acceptance (agreement) 2. consideration 3. an intention to create legal relations 4. legal capacity 5. formalities In civil-law systems, the concept of consideration is not central. In addition, for some contracts formalities must be complied with under what is sometimes called a statute of frauds. One of the most famous cases on forming a contract is Carlill v. Carbolic Smoke Ball Company, decided in nineteenth-century England.
Economic profit	In economics, Economic profit is the difference between a company"s total revenue and its opportunity costs. It is the increase in wealth that an investor has from making an investment, taking into consideration all costs associated with that investment including the opportunity cost of capital. Normal profit is a component of the firm"s opportunity costs.
Fixed costs	In economics, Fixed costs are business expenses that are not dependent on the activities of the business They tend to be time-related, such as salaries or rents being paid per month. This is in contrast to variable costs, which are volume-related (and are paid per quantity). In management accounting, Fixed costs are defined as expenses that do not change in proportion to the activity of a business, within the relevant period or scale of production.

Chapter 2. A REVIEW OF MICROECONOMIC THEORY

Chapter 2. A REVIEW OF MICROECONOMIC THEORY

Markets	A market is any one of a variety of different systems, institutions, procedures, social relations and infrastructures whereby persons trade, and goods and services are exchanged, forming part of the economy. It is an arrangement that allows buyers and sellers to exchange things. markets vary in size, range, geographic scale, location, types and variety of human communities, as well as the types of goods and services traded.
Market equilibrium	In economics, economic equilibrium is simply a state of the world where economic forces are balanced and in the absence of external influences the (equilibrium) values of economic variables will not change. It is the point at which quantity demanded and quantity supplied are equal. Market equilibrium, for example, refers to a condition where a market price is established through competition such that the amount of goods or services sought by buyers is equal to the amount of goods or services produced by sellers.
Variable cost	Variable costs are expenses that change in proportion to the activity of a business. In other words, Variable cost is the sum of marginal costs. It can also be considered normal costs.
Barriers to entry	In economics and mostly especially in the theory of competition, Barriers to entry are obstacles in the path of a firm that make it difficult to enter a given market. Barriers to entry are the source of a firm"s pricing power - the ability of a firm to raise prices without losing all its customers. The term refers to hindrances that an individual may face while trying to gain entrance into a profession or trade.
Industry	An industry is the manufacturing of a good or service within a category. Although industry is a broad term for any kind of economic production, in economics and urban planning industry is a synonym for the secondary sector, which is a type of economic activity involved in the manufacturing of raw materials into goods and products. There are four key industrial economic sectors: the primary sector, largely raw material extraction industries such as mining and farming; the secondary sector, involving refining, construction, and manufacturing; the tertiary sector, which deals with services and distribution of manufactured goods; and the quaternary sector, a relatively new type of knowledge industry focusing on technological research, design and development such as computer programming, and biochemistry.
Economies of scale	Economies of scale, in microeconomics, are the cost advantages that a business obtains due to expansion. They are factors that cause a producer"s average cost per unit to fall as scale is increased. Economies of scale is a long run concept and refers to reductions in unit cost as the size of a facility, or scale, increases.
Opportunity cost	Opportunity cost or economic opportunity loss is the value of the next best alternative forgone as the result of making a decision. Opportunity cost analysis is an important part of a company"s decision-making processes but is not treated as an actual cost in any financial statement. The next best thing that a person can engage in is referred to as the Opportunity cost of doing the best thing and ignoring the next best thing to be done.

Chapter 2. A REVIEW OF MICROECONOMIC THEORY

Chapter 2. A REVIEW OF MICROECONOMIC THEORY

Marginal revenue	In microeconomics, Marginal revenue is the extra revenue that an additional unit of product will bring. It is the additional income from selling one more unit of a good; sometimes equal to price. It can also be described as the change in total revenue/change in number of units sold.
Dot-com bubble	The "Dot-com bubble" (or) was a speculative bubble covering roughly 1998-2001 (with a climax on March 10, 2000 with the NASDAQ peaking at 5132.52) during which stock markets in Western nations saw their equity value rise rapidly from growth in the more recent Internet sector and related fields. While the latter part was a boom and bust cycle, the Internet boom sometimes is meant to refer to the steady commercial growth of the Internet with the advent of the world wide web as exemplified by the first release of the Mosaic web browser in 1993 and continuing through the 1990s. The period was marked by the founding (and, in many cases, spectacular failure) of a group of new Internet-based companies commonly referred to as dot-coms.
Imperfect competition	In economic theory, Imperfect competition is the competitive situation in any market where the conditions necessary for perfect competition are not satisfied. It is a market structure that does not meet the conditions of perfect competition. Forms of Imperfect competition include: · Monopoly, in which there is only one seller of a good. · Oligopoly, in which there is a small number of sellers. · Monopolistic competition, in which there are many sellers producing highly differentiated goods. · Monopsony, in which there is only one buyer of a good. · Oligopsony, in which there is a small number of buyers. There may also be Imperfect competition in markets due to buyers or sellers lacking information about prices and the goods being traded.
Oligopoly	An Oligopoly is a market form in which a market or industry is dominated by a small number of sellers (oligopolists). The word is derived, by analogy with "monopoly", from the Greek oligoi "few" and poleein "to sell". Because there are few sellers, each oligopolist is likely to be aware of the actions of the others.
Game theory	The games studied in Game theory are well-defined mathematical objects. A game consists of a set of players, a set of moves (or strategies) available to those players, and a specification of payoffs for each combination of strategies. Most cooperative games are presented in the characteristic function form, while the extensive and the normal forms are used to define noncooperative games.
Payment	A Payment is the transfer of wealth from one party (such as a person or company) to another. A Payment is usually made in exchange for the provision of goods, services or both, or to fulfill a legal obligation. The simplest and oldest form of Payment is barter, the exchange of one good or service for another.

Chapter 2. A REVIEW OF MICROECONOMIC THEORY

Chapter 2. A REVIEW OF MICROECONOMIC THEORY

Controllability	Controllability is an important property of a control system, and the Controllability property plays a crucial role in many control problems, such as stabilization of unstable systems by feedback, the concept of Controllability denotes the ability to move a system around in its entire configuration space using only certain admissible manipulations.
Nash equilibrium	In game theory, Nash equilibrium is a solution concept of a game involving two or more players, in which each player is assumed to know the equilibrium strategies of the other players, and no player has anything to gain by changing only his or her own strategy unilaterally. If each player has chosen a strategy and no player can benefit by changing his or her strategy while the other players keep theirs unchanged, then the current set of strategy choices and the corresponding payoffs constitute a Nash equilibrium. Stated simply, Amy and Bill are in Nash equilibrium if Amy is making the best decision she can, taking into account Bill"s decision, and Bill is making the best decision he can, taking into account Amy"s decision.
Asset	In business and accounting, Assets are economic resources owned by business or company. Anything tangible or intangible that one possesses, usually considered as applicable to the payment of one"s debts is considered an Asset. Simplistically stated, Assets are things of value that can be readily converted into cash (although cash itself is also considered an Asset).
Nominative determinism	Nominative determinism refers to the theory that a person"s name is given an influential role in reflecting key attributes of his job, profession, but real examples are more highly prized, the more obscure the better.
Pricing	Pricing is a fundamental aspect of financial modelling, and is one of the four Ps of the marketing mix. The other three aspects are product, promotion, and place. It is also a key variable in microeconomic price allocation theory. Price is the only revenue generating element amongst the four Ps, the rest being cost centers. Pricing is the manual or automatic process of applying prices to purchase and sales orders, based on factors such as: a fixed amount, quantity break, promotion or sales campaign, specific vendor quote, price prevailing on entry, shipment or invoice date, combination of multiple orders or lines, and many others.
Market failure	In economics, a Market failure exists when the production or use of goods and services by the market is not efficient. That is, there exists another outcome where market participants" total gains from the new outcome outweigh their losses (even if some participants lose under the new arrangement). Market failures can be viewed as scenarios where individuals" pursuit of pure self-interest leads to results that are not efficient - that can be improved upon from the societal point-of-view.
Market power	In economics, Market power is the ability of a firm to alter the market price of a good or service. A firm with Market power can raise prices without losing all customers to competitors. When a firm has Market power it faces a downward-sloping demand curve.

Chapter 2. A REVIEW OF MICROECONOMIC THEORY

Chapter 2. A REVIEW OF MICROECONOMIC THEORY

Cost	In business, retail, and accounting, a cost is the value of money that has been used up to produce something, and hence is not available for use anymore. In economics, a cost is an alternative that is given up as a result of a decision. In business, the cost may be one of acquisition, in which case the amount of money expended to acquire it is counted as cost.
External	In economics, an externality or spillover of an economic transaction is an impact on a party that is not directly involved in the transaction. In such a case, prices do not reflect the full costs or benefits in production or consumption of a product or service. An advantageous impact is called an external benefit or positive externality, while a detrimental impact is called an external cost or negative externality.
External benefit	In economics, an externality or spillover of an economic transaction is an impact on a party that is not directly involved in the transaction. In such a case, prices do not reflect the full costs or benefits in production or consumption of a product or service. An advantageous impact is called an external benefit or positive externality, while a detrimental impact is called an external cost or negative externality.
External cost	In economics, an externality or spillover of an economic transaction is an impact on a party that is not directly involved in the transaction. In such a case, prices do not reflect the full costs or benefits in production or consumption of a product or service. An advantageous impact is called an external benefit or positive externality, while a detrimental impact is called an external cost or negative externality.
Social	The term social refers to a characteristic of living organisms (humans in particular, though biologists also apply the term to populations of other animals). It always refers to the interaction of organisms with other organisms and to their collective co-existence, irrespective of whether they are aware of it or not, and irrespective of whether the interaction is voluntary or involuntary. In the absence of agreement about its meaning, the term "ps" is used in many different senses and regarded as a [[]], referringse among other things to: · Attitudes, orientations, or behaviours which take the interests, intentions, or needs of other people into account (in contrast to anti-social behaviour);has played some role in defining the idea or the principle. For instance terms like social realism, social justice, social constructivism, social psychology and social capital imply that there is some social process involved or considered, a process that is not there in regular, "non-social", realism, justice, constructivism, psychology, or capital.
Fixed tax	A Fixed tax is a lump sum tax that is not measured as a percentage of the tax base (income, wealth). Fixed taxes like a poll tax or sin tax are often considered regressive, but could have progressive effects if applied to luxury goods and services. Since citizens share common roads, military protection, policing, and other government services, some argue that citizens should pay the same amount for basic infrastructure.

Chapter 2. A REVIEW OF MICROECONOMIC THEORY

Chapter 2. A REVIEW OF MICROECONOMIC THEORY

Beneficiaries	A beneficiary (also, in trust law, referred to as the cestui que use) in the broadest sense is a natural person or other legal entity who receives money or other benefits from a benefactor. For example: The beneficiary of a life insurance policy, is the person who receives the payment of the amount of insurance after the death of the insured. The Beneficiaries of a trust are the persons with equitable ownership of the trust assets, although legal title is held by the trustee.
Cost-benefit	Cost-benefit analysis is a term that refers both to: · helping to appraise, or assess, the case for a project or proposal, which itself is a process known as project appraisal; and · an informal approach to making decisions of any kind. Under both definitions the process involves, whether explicitly or implicitly, weighing the total expected costs against the total expected benefits of one or more actions in order to choose the best or most profitable option. The formal process is often referred to as either CBA (cost-benefit Analysis) or BCA (Benefit-Cost Analysis).
Cost-benefit analysis	Cost-benefit analysis is a term that refers both to: · helping to appraise, or assess, the case for a project or proposal, which itself is a process known as project appraisal; and · an informal approach to making decisions of any kind. Under both definitions the process involves, whether explicitly or implicitly, weighing the total expected costs against the total expected benefits of one or more actions in order to choose the best or most profitable option. The formal process is often referred to as either CBA (Cost-benefit analysis) or BCA (Benefit-Cost Analysis).
Impossibility Theorem	In social choice theory, Arrow"s Impossibility theorem, demonstrates that no voting system can convert the ranked preferences of individuals into a community-wide ranking while also meeting a certain set of criteria with three or more discrete options to choose from. These criteria are called unrestricted domain, non-imposition, non-dictatorship, Pareto efficiency, and independence of irrelevant alternatives. The theorem is often cited in discussions of election theory as it is further interpreted by the Gibbard-Satterthwaite theorem.
Kaldor-Hicks efficiency	Kaldor-Hicks efficiency is a measure of economic efficiency that captures some of the intuitive appeal of Pareto efficiency, but has less stringent criteria and is hence applicable to more circumstances. Under Kaldor-Hicks efficiency, an outcome is considered more efficient if a Pareto optimal outcome can be reached by arranging sufficient compensation from those that are made better off to those that are made worse off so that all would end up no worse off than before. Under Pareto efficiency, an outcome is more efficient if at least one person is made better off and nobody is made worse off.
Negligence	Negligence is a legal concept in the common law legal systems usually used to achieve compensation for injuries (not accidents). Negligence is a type of tort or delict (also known as a civil wrong).

Chapter 2. A REVIEW OF MICROECONOMIC THEORY

Chapter 2. A REVIEW OF MICROECONOMIC THEORY

Social welfare function	In economics, a Social welfare function is a real-valued function that ranks conceivable social states (alternative complete descriptions of the society) from lowest to highest. Inputs of the function include any variables considered to affect welfare of the society (Sen, 1970, p. 33). In using welfare measures of persons in the society as inputs, the Social welfare function is individualistic in form.
Decision making	Decision making can be regarded as an outcome of mental processes (cognitive process) leading to the selection of a course of action among several alternatives. Every decision making process produces a final choice. The output can be an action or an opinion of choice.
Insurance	Insurance, in law and economics, is a form of risk management primarily used to hedge against the risk of a contingent loss. Insurance is defined as the equitable transfer of the risk of a loss, from one entity to another, in exchange for a premium, and can be thought of as a guaranteed and known small loss to prevent a large, possibly devastating loss. An insurer is a company selling the Insurance; an insured or policyholder is the person or entity buying the Insurance.
Expected utility	In economics, game theory, and decision theory the Expected utility theorem predicts that the "betting preferences" of people with regard to uncertain outcomes (gambles) can be described by a mathematical relation which takes into account the size of a payout (whether in money or other goods), the probability of occurrence, risk aversion, and the different utility of the same payout to people with different assets or personal preferences. It is a more sophisticated theory than simply predicting that choices will be made based on expected value (which takes into account only the size of the payout and the probability of occurrence). Daniel Bernoulli described the complete theory in 1738. John von Neumann and Oskar Morgenstern reinterpreted and presented an axiomatization of the same theory in 1944. They proved that any "normal" preference relation over a finite set of states can be written as an Expected utility, sometimes referred to as von Neumann-Morgenstern utility.
Risk aversion	Risk aversion is a concept in economics, finance, and psychology related to the behaviour of consumers and investors under uncertainty. Risk aversion is the reluctance of a person to accept a bargain with an uncertain payoff rather than another bargain with a more certain, but possibly lower, expected payoff. For example, a risk-averse investor might choose to put his or her money into a bank account with a low but guaranteed interest rate, rather than into a stock that is likely to have high returns, but also has a chance of becoming worthless.
Money	Money as we know it today is a symbol of value created by the human imagination with no intrinsic value of its own. A coin or paper currency note has value because people accept it as a symbolic medium of exchange. The economic value of Money as measured by its purchasing power is a subject of economic theory.

Chapter 2. A REVIEW OF MICROECONOMIC THEORY

Chapter 2. A REVIEW OF MICROECONOMIC THEORY

Marginal utility

In economics, the Marginal utility of a good or of a service is the utility of the specific use to which an agent would put a given increase in that good or service, Marginal utility is the utility of the marginal use -- which, on the assumption of economic rationality, would be the least urgent use of the good or service, from the best feasible combination of actions in which its use is included. Under the mainstream assumptions, the Marginal utility of a good or service is the posited quantified change in utility obtained by increasing or by decreasing use of that good or service.

Law of large numbers

The Law of large numbers (LLN) is a theorem in probability that describes the long-term stability of the mean of a random variable. Given a random variable with a finite expected value, if its values are repeatedly sampled, as the number of these observations increases, the sample mean will tend to approach and stay close to the expected value (the average for the population).

Loss aversion

In prospect theory, Loss aversion refers to people"s tendency to strongly prefer avoiding losses to acquiring gains. Some studies suggest that losses are twice as powerful, psychologically, as gains. Loss aversion was first convincingly demonstrated by Amos Tversky and Daniel Kahneman.

Debit card

A debit card is a plastic card that provides an alternative payment method to cash when making purchases. Functionally, it can be called an electronic cheque, as the funds are withdrawn directly from either the bank account, or from the remaining balance on the card. In some cases, the cards are designed exclusively for use on the Internet, and so there is no physical card.

Adverse selection

Adverse selection, anti-selection, insurance, statistics, and risk management. It refers to a market process in which "bad" results occur when buyers and sellers have asymmetric information (i.e. access to different information): the "bad" products or customers are more likely to be selected. A bank that sets one price for all its checking account customers runs the risk of being adversely selected against by its low-balance, high-activity (and hence least profitable) customers.

Deductible

In an insurance policy, the Deductible (North American term) or excess (UK term) is the portion of any claim that is not covered by the insurance provider. It is the amount of expenses that must be paid out of pocket before an insurer will cover any expenses. It is normally quoted as a fixed quantity and is a part of most policies covering losses to the policy holder.

Moral hazard

Moral hazard is the fact that a party insulated from risk may behave differently from the way it would behave if it would be fully exposed to the risk. In insurance, Moral hazard that occurs without conscious or malicious action is called morale hazard.

Moral hazard is a special case of information asymmetry, a situation in which one party in a transaction has more information than another.

Growth

Growth refers to an increase in some quantity over time. The quantity can be:

· Physical (e.g., growth in height, growth in an amount of money)
· Abstract (e.g., a system becoming more complex, an organism becoming more mature).

It can also refer to the mode of growth, i.e. numeric models for describing how much a particular quantity grows over time.

Chapter 2. A REVIEW OF MICROECONOMIC THEORY

Chapter 2. A REVIEW OF MICROECONOMIC THEORY

- Cell growth
- A tumour is sometimes referred to as a "growth"
- Bacterial growth
- Fungal growth
- Human development (biology)
- growth hormone
- growth "spurt" (rapid change in puberty)
- Auxology (Human development)

- Human development (humanity)
- Human development (psychology)
- Personal development ("Personal growth")
- Individual growth
- Population growth

- Economic growth
- For financial growth due to simple interest or compound interest see Interest
- growth investing

- Linear growth
- Logistic growth
- Exponential growth
- Hyperbolic growth "

Chapter 2. A REVIEW OF MICROECONOMIC THEORY

Chapter 3. AN INTRODUCTION TO LAW AND LEGAL INSTITUTIONS

Tort	Tort law is a body of law that addresses, and provides remedies for, civil wrongs not arising out of contractual obligations. A person who suffers legal damages may be able to use Tort law to receive compensation from someone who is legally responsible, or liable, for those injuries. Generally speaking, Tort law defines what constitutes a legal injury and establishes the circumstances under which one person may be held liable for another"s injury.
Code	In communications, a Code is a rule for converting a piece of information (for example, a letter, word, phrase) into another form or representation (one sign into another sign), not necessarily of the same type. In communications and information processing, encoding is the process by which information from a source is converted into symbols to be communicated. Decoding is the reverse process, converting these Code symbols back into information understandable by a receiver.
Mercantile	Mercantile (or Commercial) Agencies, is the name given in United States to organizations designed to collect, record and distribute to regular clients information relative to the standing of commercial firms. In Great Britain and some European countries trade protective societies, composed of merchants and tradesmen, are formed for the promotion of trade, and members exchange information regarding the standing of business houses. These societies had their origin in the associations formed in the middle of the 18th century for the purpose of disseminating information regarding bankruptcies, assignments and bills of sale.
Elawyering	The term Elawyering or e-lawyering is a neologism used to refer to the practice of law over the Internet, in a way more expansive than a mere legal related internet advertisement for a service, lawyer, Elawyering initiatives have been undertaken by the American Bar Association in order to reach a "latent market" of lower and middle class citizens in need of legal services. Lawyers practicing law online are also referred to as "virtual lawyers" and practice from virtual law offices.
Regulation	Regulation refers to "controlling human or societal behaviour by rules or restrictions." Regulation can take many forms: legal restrictions promulgated by a government authority, self-Regulation, social Regulation (e.g. norms), co-Regulation and market Regulation. One can consider Regulation as actions of conduct imposing sanctions (such as a fine). This action of administrative law, or implementing regulatory law, may be contrasted with statutory or case law.
Uniform Commercial Code	The Uniform Commercial Code (Uniform Commercial Code or the Code), first published in 1952, is one of a number of uniform acts that have been promulgated in conjunction with efforts to harmonize the law of sales and other commercial transactions in all 50 states within the United States of America. This objective is deemed important because of the prevalence of commercial transactions that extend beyond one state . If the Uniform Commercial Code had not been adopted, it is likely that the Congress of the United States, exercising its authority under the Commerce Clause of the United States Constitution would have enacted national legislation. The Uniform Commercial Code therefore achieved the goal of achieving substantial uniformity in commercial legislation and, at the same time, allowed the states needed flexibility to meet local circumstances.

Chapter 3. AN INTRODUCTION TO LAW AND LEGAL INSTITUTIONS

Chapter 3. AN INTRODUCTION TO LAW AND LEGAL INSTITUTIONS

Anecdotal value	In economics, Anecdotal value refers to the primarily social and political value of an anecdote or anecdotal evidence in promoting understanding of a social, cultural, in the last several decades the evaluation of anecdotes has received sustained academic scrutiny from economists and scholars such as S.G. Checkland (on David Ricardo), Steven Novella, Hollis Robbins, R. Charleton, Kwamena Kwansah-Aidoo, and others; these academics seek to quantify the value inherent in the deployment of anecdotes. More recently, economists studying choice models have begun assessing Anecdotal value in the context of framing; Kahneman and Tversky suggest that choice models may be contingent on stories or anecdotes that frame or influence choice.
Restatement	The Restatements of the Law are treatises on U.S. legal topics published by the American Law Institute, an organization of legal academics and practitioners, as scholarly refinements of black-letter law, to "address uncertainty in the law through a Restatement of basic legal subjects that would tell judges and lawyers what the law was." As Harvard Law School describes the Restatements: The ALI"s aim is to distill the "black letter law" from cases, to indicate a trend in common law, and, occasionally, to recommend what a rule of law should be. In essence, they restate existing common law into a series of principles or rules. While considered secondary authority (compare to primary authority), the authoritativeness of the Restatements of the Law is evidenced by their acceptance by courts throughout the United States.
Hierarchy	A hierarchy is an arrangement of items (objects, names, values, categories, etc). in which the items are represented as being "above," "below," or "at the same level as" one another and with only one "neighbour" above and below each level. These classifications are made with regard to rank, importance, seniority, power status or authority.
Rights	Rights are entitlements or permissions, usually of a legal or moral nature. rights are of vital importance in the fields of law and ethics, especially theories of justice and deontology. There are numerous different theoretical distinctions in accordance with which rights may be classified.
State court	In the United States, a State court has jurisdiction over disputes with some connection to a U.S. state. Cases are heard before and evidence is presented in a trial court, which is usually located in a courthouse in the county seat. Territory outside of any state in the United States, such as the District of Columbia or American Samoa, often have courts established under federal or territorial law which substitute for a State court system, distinct from the ordinary federal court system.
Trial	In law, a trial is when parties come together to a dispute present information (in the form of evidence) in a formal setting, usually a court, before a judge, jury, in order to achieve a resolution to their dispute. · Where the trial is held before a group of members of the community, it is called a jury trial. · Where the trial is held solely before a judge, it is called a bench trial. Bench trials involve fewer formalities, and are typically resolved faster. Furthermore, a favorable ruling for one party in a bench trial will frequently lead the other party to offer a settlement.

Chapter 3. AN INTRODUCTION TO LAW AND LEGAL INSTITUTIONS

Chapter 3. AN INTRODUCTION TO LAW AND LEGAL INSTITUTIONS

Trial court	A Trial court or court of first instance is a court in which trials take place. A Trial court of general jurisdiction is authorized to hear any type of civil or criminal case that is not committed exclusively to another court. In the United States, the United States district courts are the Trial courts of general jurisdiction of the federal judiciary; each U.S. state has a state court systems establishing Trial courts of general jurisdiction, such as the Florida Circuit Courts in Florida, the Superior Courts of California in California, and the New York Supreme Court in New York.
United States	The United States of America (commonly referred to as the United States, the U.S., the USA) is a federal constitutional republic comprising fifty states and a federal district. The country is situated mostly in central North America, where its forty-eight contiguous states and Washington, D.C., the capital district, lie between the Pacific and Atlantic Oceans, bordered by Canada to the north and Mexico to the south. The state of Alaska is in the northwest of the continent, with Canada to the east and Russia to the west across the Bering Strait.
Nominative determinism	Nominative determinism refers to the theory that a person"s name is given an influential role in reflecting key attributes of his job, profession, but real examples are more highly prized, the more obscure the better.
Liability	In financial accounting, a Liability is defined as an obligation of an entity arising from past transactions or events, the settlement of which may result in the transfer or use of assets, provision of services or other yielding of economic benefits in the future. · All type of borrowing from persons or banks for improving a business or person income which is payable during short or long time. · They embody a duty or responsibility to others that entails settlement by future transfer or use of assets, provision of services or other yielding of economic benefits, at a specified or determinable date, on occurrence of a specified event, or on demand; · The duty or responsibility obligates the entity leaving it little or no discretion to avoid it; and, · The transaction or event obligating the entity has already occurred. Liabilities in financial accounting need not be legally enforceable; but can be based on equitable obligations or constructive obligations. An equitable obligation is a duty based on ethical or moral considerations.
Supreme Court	A Supreme Court (, court of final appeal or high court) is in some jurisdictions the highest judicial body within that jurisdiction"s court system, whose rulings are not subject to further review by another court. The designations for such courts differ among jurisdictions. Courts of last resort typically function primarily as appellate courts, hearing appeals from the lower trial courts or intermediate-level appellate courts.
Appeal	In law, an appeal is a process for requesting a formal change to an official decision. The specific procedures for appealing, including even whether there is a right of appeal from a particular type of decision, can vary greatly from country to country. Even within a jurisdiction, the nature of an appeal can vary greatly depending on the type of case.

Chapter 3. AN INTRODUCTION TO LAW AND LEGAL INSTITUTIONS

Chapter 3. AN INTRODUCTION TO LAW AND LEGAL INSTITUTIONS

Intellectual property	Intellectual property is a number of distinct types of legal monopolies over creations of the mind, both artistic and commercial, and the corresponding fields of law. Under Intellectual property law, owners are granted certain exclusive rights to a variety of intangible assets, such as musical, literary, and artistic works; ideas, discoveries and inventions; and words, phrases, symbols, and designs. Common types of Intellectual property include copyrights, trademarks, patents, industrial design rights and trade secrets in some jurisdictions.
Dot-com bubble	The "Dot-com bubble" (or) was a speculative bubble covering roughly 1998-2001 (with a climax on March 10, 2000 with the NASDAQ peaking at 5132.52) during which stock markets in Western nations saw their equity value rise rapidly from growth in the more recent Internet sector and related fields. While the latter part was a boom and bust cycle, the Internet boom sometimes is meant to refer to the steady commercial growth of the Internet with the advent of the world wide web as exemplified by the first release of the Mosaic web browser in 1993 and continuing through the 1990s. The period was marked by the founding (and, in many cases, spectacular failure) of a group of new Internet-based companies commonly referred to as dot-coms.
Summary	A summary or recap is a shortened version of the original. The main purpose of such a simplification is to highlight the major points from the original (much longer) subject, e.g. a text, a film or an event. The target is to help the audience get the gist in a short period of time.
Reasonable doubt	If doubt does affect a "reasonable person"s" belief that the defendant is guilty, the jury is not satisfied beyond a "Reasonable doubt". The precise meaning of words such as "reasonable" and "doubt" are usually defined within jurisprudence of the applicable country. The use of "Reasonable doubt" as a standard requirement in the western justice system originated in medieval England.
Contributory negligence	Contributory negligence is a common law defense to a claim based on negligence, an action in tort. It applies to cases where a plaintiff has, through his own negligence, contributed to the harm he suffered. For example, a pedestrian crosses a road negligently and is hit by a driver who was driving negligently.

Chapter 3. AN INTRODUCTION TO LAW AND LEGAL INSTITUTIONS

Chapter 4. AN ECONOMIC THEORY OF PROPERTY

Anecdotal value	In economics, Anecdotal value refers to the primarily social and political value of an anecdote or anecdotal evidence in promoting understanding of a social, cultural, in the last several decades the evaluation of anecdotes has received sustained academic scrutiny from economists and scholars such as S.G. Checkland (on David Ricardo), Steven Novella, Hollis Robbins, R. Charleton, Kwamena Kwansah-Aidoo, and others; these academics seek to quantify the value inherent in the deployment of anecdotes. More recently, economists studying choice models have begun assessing Anecdotal value in the context of framing; Kahneman and Tversky suggest that choice models may be contingent on stories or anecdotes that frame or influence choice.
Casualty insurance	Casualty insurance is a problematically defined term loosely used to describe an area of insurance not particularly or directly concerned with life insurance, health insurance, and is mainly used to describe the liability coverage of an individual or organization"s for negligent acts or omissions. However, the "elastic" term has also been used to describe property insurance for aviation insurance, boiler and machinery insurance, and glass and crime insurance.
Possession	The word Possession might refer to: · Possession (1981 film), starring Sam Neill, Isabelle Adjani; dir. by Andrzej Zulawski · Possession (2002 film), adaptation of the A. S. Byatt novel; with Aaron Eckhart and Gwyneth Paltrow · Possession (2009 film), starring Sarah Michelle Gellar and Lee Pace · Possession (TV series), 1985 Australian series · Possession (video game), a possibly cancelled console game · Possession (Iron Butterfly song), song by American psychedelic rock band Iron Butterfly · Possession , a 1989 song and one of the singles taken from Bad English"s self-titled debut album · Possession , a 1993 song by Sarah McLachlan on her album Fumbling Towards Ecstasy · "Possession", song on the 2005 Mandaryna.com2me album by the Polish singer Mandaryna · "Possession", a song by death metal band Whitechapel · La Possession, French commune on the Indian Ocean island of Réunion · Possession Point, former land form, Hong Kong · Possession Sound, Washington state · Possession Street, Hong Kong · Dependent territory, an area of land over which another country exercises sovereignty, but which does not have the full right of participation in that country"s governance · Ownership · Possession (law), exclusive practical control of a thing, in the context of the legal implications of that control · Title (property) · Drug Possession, a crime · Inalienable Possession, relationship between two objects that is irreversible · Possession (linguistics), grammatically expressed relationship such as control-of and ownership-of · Possession (novel), 1990 novel by A. S. Byatt

Chapter 4. AN ECONOMIC THEORY OF PROPERTY

Chapter 4. AN ECONOMIC THEORY OF PROPERTY

	· Demonic Possession, belief in the control of a person by the Devil or other malevolent spirit · Spirit Possession, belief in the control of the behavior of a living thing or natural object by a spiritual being .
Rights	Rights are entitlements or permissions, usually of a legal or moral nature. rights are of vital importance in the fields of law and ethics, especially theories of justice and deontology. There are numerous different theoretical distinctions in accordance with which rights may be classified.
Cooperative	A cooperative (also co-operative or coöperative; often referred to as a co-op or coop) is defined by the International Co-operative Alliance"s Statement on the Co-operative Identity as an autonomous association of persons united voluntarily to meet their common economic, social, and cultural needs and aspirations through a jointly-owned and democratically-controlled enterprise. It is a business organization owned and operated by a group of individuals for their mutual benefit. A cooperative may also be defined as a business owned and controlled equally by the people who use its services or who work at it.
Non-cooperative game	In game theory, a non-cooperative game is a one in which players make decisions independently. Thus, while they may be able to cooperate, any cooperation must be self-enforcing. A game in which players can enforce contracts through third parties is a cooperative game.
Solution	In chemistry, a Solution is a homogeneous mixture composed of two or more substances. In such a mixture, a solute is dissolved in another substance, known as a solvent. Gases may dissolve in liquids, for example, carbon dioxide or oxygen in water.
Elawyering	The term Elawyering or e-lawyering is a neologism used to refer to the practice of law over the Internet, in a way more expansive than a mere legal related internet advertisement for a service, lawyer, Elawyering initiatives have been undertaken by the American Bar Association in order to reach a "latent market" of lower and middle class citizens in need of legal services. Lawyers practicing law online are also referred to as "virtual lawyers" and practice from virtual law offices.
Bargaining	Bargaining or haggling is a type of negotiation in which the buyer and seller of a good or service dispute the price which will be paid and the exact nature of the transaction that will take place, and eventually come to an agreement. Bargaining is an alternative pricing strategy to fixed prices. Optimally, if it costs the retailer nothing to engage and allow Bargaining, he can divine the buyer"s willingness to spend.
Contract	In common-law systems, the five key requirements for the creation of a contract are: 1. offer and acceptance (agreement) 2. consideration 3. an intention to create legal relations 4. legal capacity 5. formalities In civil-law systems, the concept of consideration is not central. In addition, for some contracts formalities must be complied with under what is sometimes called a statute of frauds.

Chapter 4. AN ECONOMIC THEORY OF PROPERTY

Chapter 4. AN ECONOMIC THEORY OF PROPERTY

	One of the most famous cases on forming a contract is Carlill v. Carbolic Smoke Ball Company, decided in nineteenth-century England.
Social	The term social refers to a characteristic of living organisms (humans in particular, though biologists also apply the term to populations of other animals). It always refers to the interaction of organisms with other organisms and to their collective co-existence, irrespective of whether they are aware of it or not, and irrespective of whether the interaction is voluntary or involuntary. In the absence of agreement about its meaning, the term "ps" is used in many different senses and regarded as a [[]], referringse among other things to: · Attitudes, orientations, or behaviours which take the interests, intentions, or needs of other people into account (in contrast to anti-social behaviour);has played some role in defining the idea or the principle. For instance terms like social realism, social justice, social constructivism, social psychology and social capital imply that there is some social process involved or considered, a process that is not there in regular, "non-social", realism, justice, constructivism, psychology, or capital.
Social contract	Social contract describes a broad class of theories that try to explain the ways in which people form states and/or maintain social order. The notion of the social contract implies that the people give up some rights to a government or other authority in order to receive or maintain social order through the rule of law. It can also be thought of as an agreement by the governed on a set of rules by which they are governed.
Coase Theorem	In law and economics, the Coase theorem, attributed to Ronald Coase, describes the economic efficiency of an economic allocation or outcome in the presence of externalities. The theorem states that when trade in an externality is possible and there are no transaction costs, bargaining will lead to an efficient outcome regardless of the initial allocation of property rights. In practice, obstacles to bargaining or poorly defined property rights can prevent Coasian bargaining.
Cost	In business, retail, and accounting, a cost is the value of money that has been used up to produce something, and hence is not available for use anymore. In economics, a cost is an alternative that is given up as a result of a decision. In business, the cost may be one of acquisition, in which case the amount of money expended to acquire it is counted as cost.
Transaction cost	In economics and related disciplines, a Transaction cost is a cost incurred in making an economic exchange (restated: the cost of participating in a market). For example, most people, when buying or selling a stock, must pay a commission to their broker; that commission is a Transaction cost of doing the stock deal. Or consider buying a banana from a store; to purchase the banana, your costs will be not only the price of the banana itself, but also the energy and effort it requires to find out which of the various banana products you prefer, where to get them and at what price, the cost of traveling from your house to the store and back, the time waiting in line, and the effort of the paying itself; the costs above and beyond the cost of the banana are the Transaction costs.
Income effect	In economics, the Income effect is the change in consumption resulting from a change in real income.

Chapter 4. AN ECONOMIC THEORY OF PROPERTY

Chapter 4. AN ECONOMIC THEORY OF PROPERTY

	Another important item that can change is the money income of the consumer. The Income effect is the phenomenon observed through changes in purchasing power.
Price	Price in economics and business is the result of an exchange and from that trade we assign a numerical monetary value to a good, service or asset. If Alice trades Bob 4 apples for an orange, the price of an orange is 4 apples. Inversely, the price of an apple is 1/4 oranges.
Endowment effect	In behavioral economics, the Endowment effect is a hypothesis that people value a good or service more once their property right to it has been established. In other words, people place a higher value on objects they own than objects that they do not. In one experiment, people demanded a higher price for a coffee mug that had been given to them but put a lower price on one they did not yet own.
Common knowledge	The assertion that something is "Common knowledge" is sometimes associated with the fallacy argumentum ad populum. The fallacy essentially warns against assuming that just because everyone believes something is true does not make it so. Misinformation is easily introduced into rumors by intermediate messengers.
Search costs	Search costs are one facet of transaction costs or switching costs. Rational consumers will continue to search for a better product or service until the marginal cost of searching exceeds the marginal benefit. Search theory is a branch of microeconomics that studies decisions of this type.
Information	Information as a concept has many meanings, from everyday usage to technical settings. The concept of Information is closely related to notions of constraint, communication, control, data, form, instruction, knowledge, meaning, mental stimulus, pattern, perception, and representation. The English word was apparently derived from the Latin accusative form of the nominative (informatio): this noun is in its turn derived from the verb "informare" (to inform) in the sense of "to give form to the mind", "to discipline", "instruct", "teach": "Men so wise should go and inform their kings." (1330) Inform itself comes from the Latin verb informare, to give form to, to form an idea of.
Personal property	Personal property is a type of property. In the common law systems Personal property may also be called chattels. It is distinguished from real property, or real estate.
Factor	A factor or limiting resource is a factor that controls a process, such as organism growth or species population, size, or distribution. The availability of food, predation pressure, or availability of shelter are examples of factors that could be limiting for an organism. An example of a limiting factor is sunlight, which is crucial in rainforests.
Normative	Normative has specialized meanings in several academic disciplines. Generically, it means relating to an ideal standard or model. In practice, it has strong connotations of relating to a typical standard or model.

Chapter 4. AN ECONOMIC THEORY OF PROPERTY

Chapter 4. AN ECONOMIC THEORY OF PROPERTY

Authorization hold	Authorization hold (also card authorisation, preauthorization) is the practice within the banking industry of authorizing electronic transactions done with a debit card or credit card and holding this balance as unavailable either until the merchant clears the transaction , or the hold "falls off." In the case of debit cards, Authorization holds can fall off the account (thus rendering the balance available again) anywhere from 1-5 days after the transaction date depending on the bank"s policy; in the case of credit cards, holds may last as long as 30 days, depending on the issuing bank. Signature-based (non-PIN-based) credit and debit card transactions are a two-step process, consisting of an authorization and a settlement. When a merchant swipes a customer"s credit card, the credit card terminal connects to the merchant"s acquirer, or credit card processor, which verifies that the customer"s account is valid and that sufficient funds are available to cover the transaction"s cost.
Dot-com bubble	The "Dot-com bubble" (or) was a speculative bubble covering roughly 1998-2001 (with a climax on March 10, 2000 with the NASDAQ peaking at 5132.52) during which stock markets in Western nations saw their equity value rise rapidly from growth in the more recent Internet sector and related fields. While the latter part was a boom and bust cycle, the Internet boom sometimes is meant to refer to the steady commercial growth of the Internet with the advent of the world wide web as exemplified by the first release of the Mosaic web browser in 1993 and continuing through the 1990s. The period was marked by the founding (and, in many cases, spectacular failure) of a group of new Internet-based companies commonly referred to as dot-coms.
Damages	In law, Damages are money claimed by or ordered to be paid to a person as compensation for loss or injury. Compensatory Damages, also called actual Damages, are paid to compensate the claimant for loss, injury, or harm suffered by another"s breach of duty. On a breach of contract by a defendant, a court generally awards the sum that would restore the injured party to the economic position they expected from performance of the promise or promises (known as an "expectation measure" or "benefit-of-the-bargain" measure of Damages).
Injunction	An Injunction is an equitable remedy in the form of a court order, whereby a party is required to do, certain acts. The party that fails to adhere to the Injunction faces civil or criminal penalties and may have to pay damages or accept sanctions for failing to follow the court"s order. In some cases, breaches of Injunctions are considered serious criminal offences that merit arrest and possible prison sentences.
Money	Money as we know it today is a symbol of value created by the human imagination with no intrinsic value of its own. A coin or paper currency note has value because people accept it as a symbolic medium of exchange. The economic value of Money as measured by its purchasing power is a subject of economic theory.
Liability	In financial accounting, a Liability is defined as an obligation of an entity arising from past transactions or events, the settlement of which may result in the transfer or use of assets, provision of services or other yielding of economic benefits in the future.

Chapter 4. AN ECONOMIC THEORY OF PROPERTY

Chapter 4. AN ECONOMIC THEORY OF PROPERTY

· All type of borrowing from persons or banks for improving a business or person income which is payable during short or long time.
· They embody a duty or responsibility to others that entails settlement by future transfer or use of assets, provision of services or other yielding of economic benefits, at a specified or determinable date, on occurrence of a specified event, or on demand;
· The duty or responsibility obligates the entity leaving it little or no discretion to avoid it; and,
· The transaction or event obligating the entity has already occurred.
Liabilities in financial accounting need not be legally enforceable; but can be based on equitable obligations or constructive obligations. An equitable obligation is a duty based on ethical or moral considerations.

Relief

There are three main types of Relief. The drawing of the distinction between high and low is often drawn differently, and in fact the two are very often combined in a single work - in particular most "high-Reliefs" contain sections in "low-Relief". Dashes may or may not be used in all these terms.

Distribution

Distribution in economics refers to the way total output or income is distributed among individuals or among the factors of production (labor, land, and capital) (Samuelson and Nordhaus, 2001, p. 762). In general theory and the national income and product accounts, each unit of output corresponds to a unit of income. One use of national accounts is for classifying factor incomes and measuring their respective shares, as in National Income.

Property right

A property right is the exclusive authority to determine how a resource is used, whether that resource is owned by government or by individuals. All economic goods have a property rights attribute. This attribute has three broad components

· The right to use the good
· The right to earn income from the good
· The right to transfer the good to others

The concept of property rights as used by economists and legal scholars are related but distinct. The distinction is largely seen in the economists" focus on the ability of an individual or collective to control the use of the good.

Deregulation

Deregulation is the removal or simplification of government rules and regulations that constrain the operation of market forces. Deregulation does not mean elimination of laws against fraud, but eliminating or reducing government control of how business is done, thereby moving toward a more free market. The stated rationale f is often that fewer and simpler regulations will lead to a raised level of competitiveness, therefore higher productivity, more efficiency and lower prices overall.

Chapter 4. AN ECONOMIC THEORY OF PROPERTY

Chapter 4. AN ECONOMIC THEORY OF PROPERTY

External	In economics, an externality or spillover of an economic transaction is an impact on a party that is not directly involved in the transaction. In such a case, prices do not reflect the full costs or benefits in production or consumption of a product or service. An advantageous impact is called an external benefit or positive externality, while a detrimental impact is called an external cost or negative externality.
External cost	In economics, an externality or spillover of an economic transaction is an impact on a party that is not directly involved in the transaction. In such a case, prices do not reflect the full costs or benefits in production or consumption of a product or service. An advantageous impact is called an external benefit or positive externality, while a detrimental impact is called an external cost or negative externality.
Redistribution	In economics, redistribution is the transfer of income, wealth or property from some individuals to others. Income redistribution evens the amount of income that individuals are permitted to earn, in order to correct the ineffectiveness of a market economy to remunerate based on the amount of labor expended by an individual. The objective of moderate income redistribution is to avoid the unjust equalization of incomes on one side and unjust extremes of concentration on the other sides.
Utilitarianism	Utilitarianism is the idea that moral worth of an action is determined solely by its contribution to overall utility: that is, its contribution to happiness or pleasure as summed among all people. It is thus a form of consequentialism, meaning that the moral worth of an action is determined by its outcome. Utility, the good to be maximized, has been defined by various thinkers as happiness or pleasure (versus suffering or pain), although preference utilitarians define it as the satisfaction of preferences.
Distributive	In mathematics, and in particular in abstract algebra, distributivity is a property of binary operations that generalises the distributive law from elementary algebra. For example: $2 \times (1 + 3) = (2 \times 1) + (2 \times 3)$. In the left-hand side of the above equation, the 2 multiplies the sum of 1 and 3; on the right-hand side, it multiplies the 1 and the 3 individually, with the results added afterwards.
Distributive justice	Distributive justice concerns what some consider to be socially just with respect to the allocation of goods in a society. Thus, a community in which incidental inequalities in outcome do not arise would be considered a society guided by the principles of Distributive justice. Allocation of goods takes into thought the total amount of goods to be handed out, the process on how they in the civilization are going to dispense, and the pattern of division.
Inequality	In mathematics, an inequality is a statement about the relative size or order of two objects

Chapter 4. AN ECONOMIC THEORY OF PROPERTY

Chapter 4. AN ECONOMIC THEORY OF PROPERTY

Markets	A market is any one of a variety of different systems, institutions, procedures, social relations and infrastructures whereby persons trade, and goods and services are exchanged, forming part of the economy. It is an arrangement that allows buyers and sellers to exchange things. markets vary in size, range, geographic scale, location, types and variety of human communities, as well as the types of goods and services traded.
Conservatism	In business, investment, and accounting, the principle or convention of conservatism has at least two meanings. In investment and finance, it is a strategy which aims at long-term capital appreciation with low risk. It can be characterized as moderate or cautious and is the opposite of aggressive behavior.
Origins	Philosophy Portal Economics Portal Politics Portal v · d · e In economics, Laissez-faire) means allowing industry to be free of government restriction, especially restrictions in the form of tarriffs and government monopolies. The phrase is French, literally meaning "let the people do as they please" Sometimes, but rarely, the phrase is used to describe a form of philosophic anarchism. The exact Origins of the term laissez-faire as a slogan of economic liberalism are uncertain.

Chapter 4. AN ECONOMIC THEORY OF PROPERTY

Chapter 5. TOPICS IN THE ECONOMICS OF PROPERTY LAW

Bargaining	Bargaining or haggling is a type of negotiation in which the buyer and seller of a good or service dispute the price which will be paid and the exact nature of the transaction that will take place, and eventually come to an agreement. Bargaining is an alternative pricing strategy to fixed prices. Optimally, if it costs the retailer nothing to engage and allow Bargaining, he can divine the buyer"s willingness to spend.
Copyright	Copyright is a form of intellectual property that gives the author of an original work exclusive right for a certain time period in relation to that work, including its publication, distribution and adaptation, after which time the work is said to enter the public domain. Copyright applies to any expressible form of an idea or information that is substantive and discrete and fixed in a medium. Some jurisdictions also recognize "moral rights" of the creator of a work, such as the right to be credited for the work.
Anecdotal value	In economics, Anecdotal value refers to the primarily social and political value of an anecdote or anecdotal evidence in promoting understanding of a social, cultural, in the last several decades the evaluation of anecdotes has received sustained academic scrutiny from economists and scholars such as S.G. Checkland (on David Ricardo), Steven Novella, Hollis Robbins, R. Charleton, Kwamena Kwansah-Aidoo, and others; these academics seek to quantify the value inherent in the deployment of anecdotes. More recently, economists studying choice models have begun assessing Anecdotal value in the context of framing; Kahneman and Tversky suggest that choice models may be contingent on stories or anecdotes that frame or influence choice.
Information	Information as a concept has many meanings, from everyday usage to technical settings. The concept of Information is closely related to notions of constraint, communication, control, data, form, instruction, knowledge, meaning, mental stimulus, pattern, perception, and representation. The English word was apparently derived from the Latin accusative form of the nominative (informatio): this noun is in its turn derived from the verb "informare" (to inform) in the sense of "to give form to the mind", "to discipline", "instruct", "teach": "Men so wise should go and inform their kings." (1330) Inform itself comes from the Latin verb informare, to give form to, to form an idea of.
Information economics	Information economics or the economics of information is a branch of microeconomic theory that studies how information affects an economy and economic decisions. Information has special characteristics. It is easy to create but hard to trust.
Intellectual property	Intellectual property is a number of distinct types of legal monopolies over creations of the mind, both artistic and commercial, and the corresponding fields of law. Under Intellectual property law, owners are granted certain exclusive rights to a variety of intangible assets, such as musical, literary, and artistic works; ideas, discoveries and inventions; and words, phrases, symbols, and designs. Common types of Intellectual property include copyrights, trademarks, patents, industrial design rights and trade secrets in some jurisdictions.

Chapter 5. TOPICS IN THE ECONOMICS OF PROPERTY LAW

Chapter 5. TOPICS IN THE ECONOMICS OF PROPERTY LAW

Intellectual property law	Intellectual property (IP) is a number of distinct types of legal monopolies over creations of the mind, both artistic and commercial, and the corresponding fields of law. Under intellectual property law, owners are granted certain exclusive rights to a variety of intangible assets, such as musical, literary, and artistic works; ideas, discoveries and inventions; and words, phrases, symbols, and designs. Common types of intellectual property include copyrights, trademarks, patents, industrial design rights and trade secrets in some jurisdictions.
Patent	Patents are legal instruments intended to encourage innovation by providing a limited "monopoly" to the inventor (or their assignee) in return for the disclosure of the invention. The underlying assumption being innovation is encouraged because an inventor can secure exclusive rights, and therefore a higher probability of financial rewards in the market place. The publication of the invention is mandatory to get a Patent.
Trade	Trade is the voluntary exchange of goods, services, or both. Trade is also called commerce or transaction. A mechanism that allows Trade is called a market.
Trademark	A Trademark or trade mark is a distinctive sign or indicator used by an individual, business organization, and to distinguish its products or services from those of other entities. A Trademark is designated by the following symbols: · â„¢ (for an unregistered Trademark, that is, a mark used to promote or brand goods); · â„ (for an unregistered service mark, that is, a mark used to promote or brand services); and · Â® (for a registered Trademark). A Trademark is a type of intellectual property, and typically a name, word, phrase, logo, symbol, design, image, or a combination of these elements.
Credibility	Credibility refers to the objective and subjective components of the believability of a source or message. Traditionally, credibility has two key components: trustworthiness and expertise, which both have objective and subjective components. Trustworthiness is a based more on subjective factors, but can include objective measurements such as established reliability.
Economic growth	Economic growth is an increase in activity in an economy. It is often measured as the rate of change of gross domestic product (GDP). Economic growth refers only to the quantity of goods and services produced; it says nothing about the way in which they are produced.
Elasticity	In economics, elasticity is the ratio of the percent change in one variable to the percent change in another variable. It is a tool for measuring the responsiveness of a function to changes in parameters in a relative way. Commonly analyzed are elasticity of substitution, price and wealth.
Inelastic demand	Perfectly inelastic demand Perfectly elastic demand

Chapter 5. TOPICS IN THE ECONOMICS OF PROPERTY LAW

Chapter 5. TOPICS IN THE ECONOMICS OF PROPERTY LAW

	A price fall usually results in an increase in the quantity demanded by consumers. The demand for a good is relatively inelastic when the change in quantity demanded is less than change in price. Goods and services for which no substitutes exist are generally inelastic.
Life	Life (cf. biota) is a characteristic that distinguishes objects that have self-sustaining biological processes from those that do not --either because such functions have ceased (death), or else because they lack such functions and are classified as "inanimate." In biology, the science of living organisms, "Life" is the condition which distinguishes active organisms from inorganic matter, including the capacity for growth, functional activity and the continual change preceding death. A diverse array of living organisms (Life forms) can be found in the biosphere on Earth, and properties common to these organisms--plants, animals, fungi, protists, archaea, and bacteria -- are a carbon- and water-based cellular form with complex organization and heritable genetic information.
Characteristic	Characteristic has several particular meanings: · in mathematics. · characteristic function · Euler characteristic · characteristic (algebra) · characteristic subgroup · method of characteristics (partial differential equations) · in physics and engineering · any characteristic curve that shows the relationship between certain input- and output parameters, e.g. · an I-V or current-voltage characteristic is the current in a circuit as a function of the applied voltage · Receiver-Operator characteristic · in navigation, the characteristic pattern of a lighted beacon. · in fiction · in Dungeons ' Dragons, characteristic is another name for ability score
Trial	In law, a trial is when parties come together to a dispute present information (in the form of evidence) in a formal setting, usually a court, before a judge, jury, in order to achieve a resolution to their dispute. · Where the trial is held before a group of members of the community, it is called a jury trial. · Where the trial is held solely before a judge, it is called a bench trial. Bench trials involve fewer formalities, and are typically resolved faster. Furthermore, a favorable ruling for one party in a bench trial will frequently lead the other party to offer a settlement.
Personal property	Personal property is a type of property. In the common law systems Personal property may also be called chattels. It is distinguished from real property, or real estate.

Chapter 5. TOPICS IN THE ECONOMICS OF PROPERTY LAW

Chapter 5. TOPICS IN THE ECONOMICS OF PROPERTY LAW

Dot-com bubble	The "Dot-com bubble" (or) was a speculative bubble covering roughly 1998-2001 (with a climax on March 10, 2000 with the NASDAQ peaking at 5132.52) during which stock markets in Western nations saw their equity value rise rapidly from growth in the more recent Internet sector and related fields. While the latter part was a boom and bust cycle, the Internet boom sometimes is meant to refer to the steady commercial growth of the Internet with the advent of the world wide web as exemplified by the first release of the Mosaic web browser in 1993 and continuing through the 1990s. The period was marked by the founding (and, in many cases, spectacular failure) of a group of new Internet-based companies commonly referred to as dot-coms.
Dynamic efficiency	Dynamic efficiency is a term in economics, which refers to an economy that appropriately balances short run concerns (static efficiency) with concerns in the long run (focusing on encouraging research and development). Through Dynamic efficiency, such an economy is able to further improve efficiency over time. Investments in education, research and innovation are important in this process.
Trade-off	A Trade-off is a situation that involves losing one quality or aspect of something in return for gaining another quality or aspect. It implies a decision to be made with full comprehension of both the upside and downside of a particular choice. In economics the term is expressed as opportunity cost, referring to the most preferred alternative given up.
Growth	Growth refers to an increase in some quantity over time. The quantity can be: · Physical (e.g., growth in height, growth in an amount of money) · Abstract (e.g., a system becoming more complex, an organism becoming more mature). It can also refer to the mode of growth, i.e. numeric models for describing how much a particular quantity grows over time. · Cell growth · A tumour is sometimes referred to as a "growth" · Bacterial growth · Fungal growth · Human development (biology) · growth hormone · growth "spurt" (rapid change in puberty) · Auxology (Human development) · Human development (humanity) · Human development (psychology) · Personal development ("Personal growth") · Individual growth · Population growth · Economic growth · For financial growth due to simple interest or compound interest see Interest · growth investing

Chapter 5. TOPICS IN THE ECONOMICS OF PROPERTY LAW

Chapter 5. TOPICS IN THE ECONOMICS OF PROPERTY LAW

	· Linear growth · Logistic growth · Exponential growth · Hyperbolic growth "
Royalties	Royalties (sometimes, running Royalties) are usage-based payments made by one party to another (the "licensor") for ongoing use of an asset,) right. Royalties are typically a percentage of gross or net sales derived from use of an asset or a fixed price per unit sold of an item. but there are also other modes and metrics of compensation.
Price	Price in economics and business is the result of an exchange and from that trade we assign a numerical monetary value to a good, service or asset. If Alice trades Bob 4 apples for an orange, the price of an orange is 4 apples. Inversely, the price of an apple is 1/4 oranges.
The demand	Perfectly inelastic demand Perfectly elastic demand A price fall usually results in an increase in the quantity demanded by consumers . The demand for a good is relatively inelastic when the change in quantity demanded is less than change in price. Goods and services for which no substitutes exist are generally inelastic.
Price elasticity of demand	Price elasticity of demand (PED) is defined as the measure of responsiveness in the quantity demanded for a commodity as a result of change in price of the same commodity. It is a measure of how consumers react to a change in price. In other words, it is percentage change in quantity demanded by the percentage change in price of the same commodity.
Social	The term social refers to a characteristic of living organisms (humans in particular, though biologists also apply the term to populations of other animals). It always refers to the interaction of organisms with other organisms and to their collective co-existence, irrespective of whether they are aware of it or not, and irrespective of whether the interaction is voluntary or involuntary. In the absence of agreement about its meaning, the term "ps" is used in many different senses and regarded as a [[]], referringse among other things to: · Attitudes, orientations, or behaviours which take the interests, intentions, or needs of other people into account (in contrast to anti-social behaviour);has played some role in defining the idea or the principle. For instance terms like social realism, social justice, social constructivism, social psychology and social capital imply that there is some social process involved or considered, a process that is not there in regular, "non-social", realism, justice, constructivism, psychology, or capital.

Chapter 5. TOPICS IN THE ECONOMICS OF PROPERTY LAW

Chapter 5. TOPICS IN THE ECONOMICS OF PROPERTY LAW

Entrepreneur	An entrepreneur is a person who has possession of an enterprise, and assumes significant accountability for the inherent risks and the outcome. It is an ambitious leader who combines land, labor, and capital to often create and market new goods or services. ...
Duration	In finance, the Duration of a financial asset measures the sensitivity of the asset"s price to interest rate movements. There are various definitions of Duration and derived quantities, discussed below. If not otherwise specified, "Duration" generally means the Macaulay Duration, as defined below.
Controllability	Controllability is an important property of a control system, and the Controllability property plays a crucial role in many control problems, such as stabilization of unstable systems by feedback, the concept of Controllability denotes the ability to move a system around in its entire configuration space using only certain admissible manipulations.
Macro derivative	A macro derivative or an economic derivative is a derivative that is based on a macroeconomic figure, such as consumer confidence, jobless claims, in 2002 Goldman Sachs and Deutsche Bank announced to offer their clients auctions for derivatives based on macroeconomic key figures. In 2005 Deutsche Bank left the joint project.
Competition	Co-operative Competition is based upon promoting mutual survival - "everyone wins". Adam Smith"s "invisible hand" is a process where individuals compete to improve their level of happiness but compete in a cooperative manner through peaceful exchange and without violating other people. Cooperative Competition focuses individuals/groups/organisms against the environment.
Food, Drug, and Cosmetic Act	The United States Federal Food, Drug, and Cosmetic Act , is a set of laws passed by Congress in 1938 giving authority to the U.S. Food and Drug Administration (FDA) to oversee the safety of food, drugs, and cosmetics. A principal author of this law was Royal S. Copeland, a three-term U.S. Senator from New York. In 1968, the Electronic Product Radiation Control provisions were added to the FD'C. Also in that year the FDA formed the Drug Efficacy Study Implementation (DESI) to incorporate into FD'C regulations the recommendations from a National Academy of Sciences investigation of effectiveness of previously marketed drugs.
Drug Price Competition and Patent Term Restoration Act	The Drug Price Competition and Patent Term Restoration Act, informally known as the "Hatch-Waxman Act" [Public Law 98-417], is a 1984 United States federal law which established the modern system of generic drugs. The informal name comes from the Act"s two sponsors, representative Henry Waxman of California and senator Orrin Hatch of Utah. Hatch-Waxman amended the Federal Food, Drug, and Cosmetic Act.
Orphan drug	An Orphan drug is a pharmaceutical agent that has been developed specifically to treat a rare medical condition, the condition itself being referred to as an orphan disease. The assignment of orphan status to a disease and to any drugs developed to treat it is a matter of public policy in many countries, and has resulted in medical breakthroughs that would not have otherwise been achieved due to the economics of drug research and development.

Chapter 5. TOPICS IN THE ECONOMICS OF PROPERTY LAW

Chapter 5. TOPICS IN THE ECONOMICS OF PROPERTY LAW

The Orphan drug Act (ODA) of January 1983, passed in the United States with lobbying from the National Organization for Rare Disorders, is meant to encourage pharmaceutical companies to develop drugs for diseases that have a small market: under the law, companies that develop such a drug (a drug for a disorder affecting fewer than 200,000 people in the United States) may sell it without competition for seven years, and may get clinical trial tax incentives.

Investment | Investment or investing is a term with several closely-related meanings in business management, finance and economics, related to saving or deferring consumption. Investing is the active redirection of resources: from being consumed today, to creating benefits in the future; the use of assets to earn income or profit. An Investment is a choice by an individual or an organization such as a pension fund, after at least some careful analysis or thought, to place or lend money in a vehicle (e.g. property, stock securities, bonds) that has sufficiently low risk and provides the possibility of generating returns over a period of time.

Natural monopoly | In economics, a Natural monopoly occurs when, due to the economies of scale of a particular industry, the maximum efficiency of production and distribution is realized through a single supplier.
Natural monopolies arise where the largest supplier in an industry, often the first supplier in a market, has an overwhelming cost advantage over other actual or potential competitors. This tends to be the case in industries where capital costs predominate, creating economies of scale which are large in relation to the size of the market, and hence high barriers to entry; examples include water services and electricity.

Network effect | In economics and business, a Network effect is the effect that one user of a good or service has on the value of that product to other people.
The classic example is the telephone. The more people own telephones, the more valuable the telephone is to each owner.

Cost | In business, retail, and accounting, a cost is the value of money that has been used up to produce something, and hence is not available for use anymore. In economics, a cost is an alternative that is given up as a result of a decision. In business, the cost may be one of acquisition, in which case the amount of money expended to acquire it is counted as cost.

Future | Futures may mean:

· Futures contract, a tradable financial contract
· Futures exchange, a financial market where Futures contracts are traded
· Futures (magazine), an American finance magazine

· Futures studies, multidisciplinary studies of patterns to determine the likelihood of Future trends
· Futures (journal), an international Futures studies journal

· Futures (album), a 2004 release by Jimmy Eat World

· "Futures" (song), a single from the above album

Chapter 5. TOPICS IN THE ECONOMICS OF PROPERTY LAW

Chapter 5. TOPICS IN THE ECONOMICS OF PROPERTY LAW

	· Futures and promises, computer programming objects that act as proxies for results that are not yet determined · Futures tournaments, minor professional tennis events .
Trade name	A Trade name is the name which a business trades under for commercial purposes, although its registered, legal name, used for contracts and other formal situations, may be another. Trade names are also used in retailing to make oddly named articles more appealing to customers, or to make it easier for customers to recognize a product with a technical or difficult to remember name. Trade names are informal, public domain terms, unlike trademarks.
Organization	Management is interested in Organization mainly from an instrumental point of view. For a company, Organization is a means to an end to achieve its goals. Among the theories that are or have been most influential are: · Pyramids or hierarchies · Committees or juries · Matrix Organizations · Ecologies A hierarchy exemplifies an arrangement with a leader who leads leaders. This arrangement is often associated with bureaucracy.
Trust	In common law legal systems, a Trust is an arrangement whereby property (including real, tangible and intangible) is managed by one person (or persons) for the benefit of another. A Trust is created by a settlor (or feoffor to uses), who enTrusts some or all of his property to people of his choice (the Trustees or feoffee to uses). The Trustees hold legal title to the Trust property (or Trust corpus), but they are obliged to hold the property for the benefit of one or more individuals or organizations (the beneficiary, cestui que use, or cestui que Trust), usually specified by the settlor, who hold equitable title.
Governance	Governance relates to decisions that define expectations, grant power
Incentive	In economics and sociology, an Incentive is any factor (financial or non-financial) that enables or motivates a particular course of action, the study of Incentive structures is central to the study of all economic activity (both in terms of individual decision-making and in terms of co-operation and competition within a larger institutional structure).
Theory of the firm	The Theory of the firm consists of a number of economic theories which describe the nature of the firm, company, including its existence, its behaviour, and its relationship with the market. In simplified terms, the Theory of the firm aims to answer these questions:

Chapter 5. TOPICS IN THE ECONOMICS OF PROPERTY LAW

Chapter 5. TOPICS IN THE ECONOMICS OF PROPERTY LAW

· Existence - why do firms emerge, why are not all transactions in the economy mediated over the market?
· Boundaries - why the boundary between firms and the market is located exactly there? Which transactions are performed internally and which are negotiated on the market?
· Organization - why are firms structured in such a specific way? What is the interplay of formal and informal relationships?

The First World War period saw a change of emphasis in economic theory away from industry-level analysis which mainly included analysing markets to analysis at the level of the firm, as it became increasingly clear that perfect competition was no longer an adequate model of how firms behaved. Economic theory till then had focused on trying to understand markets alone and there had been little study on understanding why firms or organisations exist. Markets are mainly guided by prices as illustrated by vegetable markets where a buyer is free to switch sellers in an exchange.

Markets	A market is any one of a variety of different systems, institutions, procedures, social relations and infrastructures whereby persons trade, and goods and services are exchanged, forming part of the economy. It is an arrangement that allows buyers and sellers to exchange things. markets vary in size, range, geographic scale, location, types and variety of human communities, as well as the types of goods and services traded.
Market manipulation	Market manipulation describes a deliberate attempt to interfere with the free and fair operation of the market and create artificial, false or misleading appearances with respect to the price of, a security, commodity or currency. Market manipulation is prohibited in the United States under Section 9(a)(2) of the Securities Exchange Act of 1934, and in Australia under Section s 1041A of the Corporations Act 2001. The Act defines Market manipulation as transactions which create an artificial price or maintain an artificial price for a tradable security. Market manipulation can occur in multiple ways: Pools "Agreements, often written, among a group of traders to delegate authority to a single manager to trade in a specific stock for a specific period of time and then to share in the resulting profits or losses." Churning "When a trader places both buy and sell orders at about the same price.
Limited liability	Limited liability is a concept whereby a person"s financial liability is limited to a fixed sum, most commonly the value of a person"s investment in a company or partnership with Limited liability. In other words, if a company with Limited liability is sued, then the plaintiffs are suing the company, not its owners or investors. A shareholder in a limited company is not personally liable for any of the debts of the company, other than for the value of his investment in that company.
Property right	A property right is the exclusive authority to determine how a resource is used, whether that resource is owned by government or by individuals. All economic goods have a property rights attribute. This attribute has three broad components

Chapter 5. TOPICS IN THE ECONOMICS OF PROPERTY LAW

Chapter 5. TOPICS IN THE ECONOMICS OF PROPERTY LAW

· The right to use the good
· The right to earn income from the good
· The right to transfer the good to others

The concept of property rights as used by economists and legal scholars are related but distinct. The distinction is largely seen in the economists" focus on the ability of an individual or collective to control the use of the good.

Rights

Rights are entitlements or permissions, usually of a legal or moral nature. rights are of vital importance in the fields of law and ethics, especially theories of justice and deontology.

There are numerous different theoretical distinctions in accordance with which rights may be classified.

Communism

Communism is a family of economic and political ideas and social movements related to the establishment of an egalitarian, classless and stateless society based on common ownership and control of the means of production and property in general, as well as the name given to such a society. As an ideology, Communism is defined as "the doctrine of the conditions of the liberation of the proletariat". The term "Communism", when spelled with a capital letter C, however, refers to any state or political party that declares allegiance to Marxism-Leninism or a derivative thereof and explicitly identifies itself as Communist, even if that party or state is committed to non-communist economic policies; as is the case with the modern Chinese Communist Party.

Park

A park is a protected area, in its natural or semi-natural state or planted, and set aside for human recreation and enjoyment. It may consist of, rocks, soil, water, flora and fauna and grass areas.
Wilderness parks are intact and undeveloped areas used mainly by wild species.

Cooperative

A cooperative (also co-operative or coöperative; often referred to as a co-op or coop) is defined by the International Co-operative Alliance"s Statement on the Co-operative Identity as an autonomous association of persons united voluntarily to meet their common economic, social, and cultural needs and aspirations through a jointly-owned and democratically-controlled enterprise. It is a business organization owned and operated by a group of individuals for their mutual benefit. A cooperative may also be defined as a business owned and controlled equally by the people who use its services or who work at it.

Possession

The word Possession might refer to:

Chapter 5. TOPICS IN THE ECONOMICS OF PROPERTY LAW

Chapter 5. TOPICS IN THE ECONOMICS OF PROPERTY LAW

- Possession (1981 film), starring Sam Neill, Isabelle Adjani; dir. by Andrzej Zulawski
- Possession (2002 film), adaptation of the A. S. Byatt novel; with Aaron Eckhart and Gwyneth Paltrow
- Possession (2009 film), starring Sarah Michelle Gellar and Lee Pace
- Possession (TV series), 1985 Australian series
- Possession (video game), a possibly cancelled console game
- Possession (Iron Butterfly song), song by American psychedelic rock band Iron Butterfly
- Possession , a 1989 song and one of the singles taken from Bad English"s self-titled debut album
- Possession , a 1993 song by Sarah McLachlan on her album Fumbling Towards Ecstasy
- "Possession", song on the 2005 Mandaryna.com2me album by the Polish singer Mandaryna
- "Possession", a song by death metal band Whitechapel

- La Possession, French commune on the Indian Ocean island of Réunion
- Possession Point, former land form, Hong Kong
- Possession Sound, Washington state
- Possession Street, Hong Kong

- Dependent territory, an area of land over which another country exercises sovereignty, but which does not have the full right of participation in that country"s governance
- Ownership
- Possession (law), exclusive practical control of a thing, in the context of the legal implications of that control
- Title (property)
- Drug Possession, a crime

- Inalienable Possession, relationship between two objects that is irreversible
- Possession (linguistics), grammatically expressed relationship such as control-of and ownership-of

- Possession (novel), 1990 novel by A. S. Byatt

- Demonic Possession, belief in the control of a person by the Devil or other malevolent spirit
- Spirit Possession, belief in the control of the behavior of a living thing or natural object by a spiritual being .

Maximum sustainable yield	In population ecology and economics, Maximum sustainable yield is, theoretically, the largest yield (or catch) that can be taken from a species" stock over an indefinite period. Fundamental to the notion of sustainable harvest, the concept of Maximum sustainable yield aims to maintain the population size at the point of maximum growth rate by harvesting the individuals that would normally be added to the population, allowing the population to continue to be productive indefinitely. Under the assumption of logistic growth, resource limitation does not constrain individuals" reproductive rates when populations are small, but because there are few individuals, the overall yield is small.
Justice	Justice is the concept of moral rightness based on ethics, rationality, law, natural law, fairness, religion and/or equity.

Chapter 5. TOPICS IN THE ECONOMICS OF PROPERTY LAW

Chapter 5. TOPICS IN THE ECONOMICS OF PROPERTY LAW

	Justice... concerns the proper ordering of things and persons within a society.
Common ownership	Common ownership is a principle according to which the assets of an enterprise or other organization are held indivisibly rather than in the names of the individual members or by the government. Thus, rather than being "owners" of the enterprise, its members are held to be trustees of it and its assets for future generations. Common ownership is a way of "neutralising" capital, and vesting control of an enterprise by virtue of participation in it, rather than by the injection of capital.
Elawyering	The term Elawyering or e-lawyering is a neologism used to refer to the practice of law over the Internet, in a way more expansive than a mere legal related internet advertisement for a service, lawyer, Elawyering initiatives have been undertaken by the American Bar Association in order to reach a "latent market" of lower and middle class citizens in need of legal services. Lawyers practicing law online are also referred to as "virtual lawyers" and practice from virtual law offices.
Estoppel	Estoppel is a legal doctrine at common law, where a party is barred from claiming or denying an argument on an equitable ground. Estoppel complements the requirement of consideration in contract law. In general, Estoppel protects an aggrieved party, if the counter-party induced an expectation from the aggrieved party, and the aggrieved party reasonably relied on the expectation and would suffer detriment if the expectation is not met.
Statute	A statute is a formal written enactment of a legislative authority that governs a country, state, city, or county. Typically, statutes command or prohibit something, or declare policy. The word is often used to distinguish law made by legislative bodies from case law and the regulations issued by Government agencies.
Bequest	A Bequest is the act of receiving property by will. Strictly, "Bequest" is used of personal property, and "devise" of real property. It means the same thing as bequeath in legal terminology.
Inheritance	Inheritance is the practice of passing on property, titles, debts, and obligations upon the death of an individual. It has long played an important role in human societies. The rules of Inheritance differ between societies and have changed over time.
Contract	In common-law systems, the five key requirements for the creation of a contract are: 1. offer and acceptance (agreement) 2. consideration 3. an intention to create legal relations 4. legal capacity 5. formalities In civil-law systems, the concept of consideration is not central. In addition, for some contracts formalities must be complied with under what is sometimes called a statute of frauds. One of the most famous cases on forming a contract is Carlill v. Carbolic Smoke Ball Company, decided in nineteenth-century England.

Chapter 5. TOPICS IN THE ECONOMICS OF PROPERTY LAW

Chapter 5. TOPICS IN THE ECONOMICS OF PROPERTY LAW

Donation	A Donation is a gift given by physical or legal persons, typically for charitable purposes and/or to benefit a cause. A Donation may take various forms, including cash, services, new or used goods including clothing, toys, food, vehicles, it also may consist of emergency, relief or humanitarian aid items, development aid support, and can also relate to medical care needs as i.e. blood or organs for transplant. Charitable gifts of goods or services are also called gifts in kind.
Breach of contract	Breach of contract is a legal concept in which a binding agreement or bargained-for exchange is not honored by one or more of the parties to the contract by non-performance or interference with the other party"s performance. A minor breach, a partial breach or an immaterial breach, occurs when the non-breaching party is unentitled to an order for performance of its obligations, but only to collect the actual amount of their damages. For example, suppose a homeowner hires a contractor to install new plumbing and insists that the pipes, which will ultimately be sealed behind the walls, be red.
Zoning	Zoning is a device of land use regulation used by local governments in most developed countries . Zoning may be use-based , or it may regulate building height, lot coverage, and similar characteristics, or some combination of these. Theoretically, the primary purpose of Zoning is to segregate uses that are thought to be incompatible.
Regulation	Regulation refers to "controlling human or societal behaviour by rules or restrictions." Regulation can take many forms: legal restrictions promulgated by a government authority, self-Regulation, social Regulation (e.g. norms), co-Regulation and market Regulation. One can consider Regulation as actions of conduct imposing sanctions (such as a fine). This action of administrative law, or implementing regulatory law, may be contrasted with statutory or case law.
Damages	In law, Damages are money claimed by or ordered to be paid to a person as compensation for loss or injury. Compensatory Damages, also called actual Damages, are paid to compensate the claimant for loss, injury, or harm suffered by another"s breach of duty. On a breach of contract by a defendant, a court generally awards the sum that would restore the injured party to the economic position they expected from performance of the promise or promises (known as an "expectation measure" or "benefit-of-the-bargain" measure of Damages).
Injunction	An Injunction is an equitable remedy in the form of a court order, whereby a party is required to do, certain acts. The party that fails to adhere to the Injunction faces civil or criminal penalties and may have to pay damages or accept sanctions for failing to follow the court"s order. In some cases, breaches of Injunctions are considered serious criminal offences that merit arrest and possible prison sentences.
Eminent domain	

Chapter 5. TOPICS IN THE ECONOMICS OF PROPERTY LAW

Chapter 5. TOPICS IN THE ECONOMICS OF PROPERTY LAW

Eminent domain (United States), compulsory purchase (United Kingdom, New Zealand, Ireland), resumption/compulsory acquisition (Australia) or expropriation (South Africa and Canada"s common law systems) is the inherent power of the state to seize a citizen"s private property, expropriate property or seize a citizen"s rights in property with due monetary compensation, but without the owner"s consent. The property is taken either for government use or by delegation to third parties who will devote it to public or civic use or, in some cases, economic development. The most common uses of property taken by Eminent domain are for public utilities, highways, and railroads.

Insurance

Insurance, in law and economics, is a form of risk management primarily used to hedge against the risk of a contingent loss. Insurance is defined as the equitable transfer of the risk of a loss, from one entity to another, in exchange for a premium, and can be thought of as a guaranteed and known small loss to prevent a large, possibly devastating loss. An insurer is a company selling the Insurance; an insured or policyholder is the person or entity buying the Insurance.

Authorization hold

Authorization hold (also card authorisation, preauthorization) is the practice within the banking industry of authorizing electronic transactions done with a debit card or credit card and holding this balance as unavailable either until the merchant clears the transaction , or the hold "falls off." In the case of debit cards, Authorization holds can fall off the account (thus rendering the balance available again) anywhere from 1-5 days after the transaction date depending on the bank"s policy; in the case of credit cards, holds may last as long as 30 days, depending on the issuing bank.

Signature-based (non-PIN-based) credit and debit card transactions are a two-step process, consisting of an authorization and a settlement.

When a merchant swipes a customer"s credit card, the credit card terminal connects to the merchant"s acquirer, or credit card processor, which verifies that the customer"s account is valid and that sufficient funds are available to cover the transaction"s cost.

Flood insurance

Flood insurance denotes the specific insurance coverage against property loss from flooding. To determine risk factors for specific properties, insurers will often refer to topographical maps that denote lowlands and floodplains that are susceptible to flooding.

Nationwide, only 20% of American homes at risk for floods are covered by Flood insurance.

Chapter 5. TOPICS IN THE ECONOMICS OF PROPERTY LAW

Chapter 6. AN ECONOMIC THEORY OF CONTRACT

Contract	In common-law systems, the five key requirements for the creation of a contract are: 1. offer and acceptance (agreement) 2. consideration 3. an intention to create legal relations 4. legal capacity 5. formalities In civil-law systems, the concept of consideration is not central. In addition, for some contracts formalities must be complied with under what is sometimes called a statute of frauds. One of the most famous cases on forming a contract is Carlill v. Carbolic Smoke Ball Company, decided in nineteenth-century England.
Bargaining	Bargaining or haggling is a type of negotiation in which the buyer and seller of a good or service dispute the price which will be paid and the exact nature of the transaction that will take place, and eventually come to an agreement. Bargaining is an alternative pricing strategy to fixed prices. Optimally, if it costs the retailer nothing to engage and allow Bargaining, he can divine the buyer"s willingness to spend.
Expectation damages	Expectation damages are a form of damages available as a recourse to a breached contract. When a contracting party fails to fulfill their contractual duties, which causes losses to the other party, the party in breach can be liable for the losses of the other party. Losses that relate to the consequences of breach are Expectation damages, because the purpose of this type of remedy is to put the plaintiff in the position he would have been in had the contract been fulfilled.
Criticism	This article is about criticism of, and arguments against debt. There are many arguments against debt as an instrument and institution, on a personal, family, social, corporate and governmental level. Usually these refer to conditions under which debt should not be used as a solution, e.g. to fund consumption for survival.
Code	In communications, a Code is a rule for converting a piece of information (for example, a letter, word, phrase) into another form or representation (one sign into another sign), not necessarily of the same type. In communications and information processing, encoding is the process by which information from a source is converted into symbols to be communicated. Decoding is the reverse process, converting these Code symbols back into information understandable by a receiver.
Mercantile	Mercantile (or Commercial) Agencies, is the name given in United States to organizations designed to collect, record and distribute to regular clients information relative to the standing of commercial firms. In Great Britain and some European countries trade protective societies, composed of merchants and tradesmen, are formed for the promotion of trade, and members exchange information regarding the standing of business houses. These societies had their origin in the associations formed in the middle of the 18th century for the purpose of disseminating information regarding bankruptcies, assignments and bills of sale.

Chapter 6. AN ECONOMIC THEORY OF CONTRACT

Chapter 6. AN ECONOMIC THEORY OF CONTRACT

Uniform Commercial Code	The Uniform Commercial Code (Uniform Commercial Code or the Code), first published in 1952, is one of a number of uniform acts that have been promulgated in conjunction with efforts to harmonize the law of sales and other commercial transactions in all 50 states within the United States of America. This objective is deemed important because of the prevalence of commercial transactions that extend beyond one state . If the Uniform Commercial Code had not been adopted, it is likely that the Congress of the United States, exercising its authority under the Commerce Clause of the United States Constitution would have enacted national legislation. The Uniform Commercial Code therefore achieved the goal of achieving substantial uniformity in commercial legislation and, at the same time, allowed the states needed flexibility to meet local circumstances.
Anecdotal value	In economics, Anecdotal value refers to the primarily social and political value of an anecdote or anecdotal evidence in promoting understanding of a social, cultural, in the last several decades the evaluation of anecdotes has received sustained academic scrutiny from economists and scholars such as S.G. Checkland (on David Ricardo), Steven Novella, Hollis Robbins, R. Charleton, Kwamena Kwansah-Aidoo, and others; these academics seek to quantify the value inherent in the deployment of anecdotes. More recently, economists studying choice models have begun assessing Anecdotal value in the context of framing; Kahneman and Tversky suggest that choice models may be contingent on stories or anecdotes that frame or influence choice.
Elawyering	The term Elawyering or e-lawyering is a neologism used to refer to the practice of law over the Internet, in a way more expansive than a mere legal related internet advertisement for a service, lawyer, Elawyering initiatives have been undertaken by the American Bar Association in order to reach a "latent market" of lower and middle class citizens in need of legal services. Lawyers practicing law online are also referred to as "virtual lawyers" and practice from virtual law offices.
Chief brand officer	A Chief brand officer is a relatively new executive level position at a corporation, company, organization, typically reporting directly to the CEO or board of directors. The Chief brand officer is responsible for a brand"s image, experience, and promise, and propagating it throughout all aspects of the company. The brand officer oversees marketing, advertising, design, public relations and customer service departments. The brand equity of a company is seen as becoming increasingly dependent on the role of a Chief brand officer. Companies that currently employ a Chief brand officer include: · Srinivas Kumar, Baskin-Robbins Worldwide · Michael Keller, Dairy Queen · Will Kussell, Dunkin" Brands, Inc. · Trey Hall, Boston Market Corporation · Allen Schiffenbaure, G 2 Marketing Group · Alan Bergstrom, Storyminers Inc. · Brian Igoe, Metabolix, Inc. · Phil Mcaveety, Luxury Collection · Mark I. McCallum, Brown-Forman Corporation · Phil McAveety, Starwood Hotels ' Resorts Worldwide, Inc. · Danny Meisenheimer, Souper Salad, Inc

Chapter 6. AN ECONOMIC THEORY OF CONTRACT

Chapter 6. AN ECONOMIC THEORY OF CONTRACT

Deferred	Deferred, in accrual accounting, is any account where the asset or liability is not realized until a future date (accounting period), e.g. annuities, charges, taxes, income, etc. The deferred item may be carried, dependent on type of deferral, as either an asset or liability.
Cooperation	Distinguish from Corporation. Cooperation, co-operation, or coöperation is the process of working or acting together, which can be accomplished by both intentional and non-intentional agents. In its simplest form it involves things working in harmony, side by side, while in its more complicated forms, it can involve something as complex as the inner workings of a human being or even the social patterns of a nation.
Game theory	The games studied in Game theory are well-defined mathematical objects. A game consists of a set of players, a set of moves (or strategies) available to those players, and a specification of payoffs for each combination of strategies. Most cooperative games are presented in the characteristic function form, while the extensive and the normal forms are used to define noncooperative games.
Pareto efficiency	Pareto efficiency, is an important concept in economics with broad applications in game theory, engineering and the social sciences. The term is named after Vilfredo Pareto, an Italian economist who used the concept in his studies of economic efficiency and income distribution. Informally, Pareto efficient situations are those in which any change to make any person better off is impossible without making someone else worse off.
Elasticity	In economics, elasticity is the ratio of the percent change in one variable to the percent change in another variable. It is a tool for measuring the responsiveness of a function to changes in parameters in a relative way. Commonly analyzed are elasticity of substitution, price and wealth.
Inelastic demand	Perfectly inelastic demand Perfectly elastic demand A price fall usually results in an increase in the quantity demanded by consumers . The demand for a good is relatively inelastic when the change in quantity demanded is less than change in price. Goods and services for which no substitutes exist are generally inelastic.
Information	Information as a concept has many meanings, from everyday usage to technical settings. The concept of Information is closely related to notions of constraint, communication, control, data, form, instruction, knowledge, meaning, mental stimulus, pattern, perception, and representation. The English word was apparently derived from the Latin accusative form of the nominative (informatio): this noun is in its turn derived from the verb "informare" (to inform) in the sense of "to give form to the mind", "to discipline", "instruct", "teach": "Men so wise should go and inform their kings." (1330) Inform itself comes from the Latin verb informare, to give form to, to form an idea of.
Performance	A Performance, in performing arts, generally comprises an event in which one group of people (the performer or performers) behave in a particular way for another group of people (the audience). Sometimes the dividing line between performer and the audience may become blurred, as in the example of "participatory theatre" where audience members might get involved in the production. Singing choral music, and performing in a ballet are examples.

Chapter 6. AN ECONOMIC THEORY OF CONTRACT

Chapter 6. AN ECONOMIC THEORY OF CONTRACT

Incentive	In economics and sociology, an Incentive is any factor (financial or non-financial) that enables or motivates a particular course of action, the study of Incentive structures is central to the study of all economic activity (both in terms of individual decision-making and in terms of co-operation and competition within a larger institutional structure).
Controllability	Controllability is an important property of a control system, and the Controllability property plays a crucial role in many control problems, such as stabilization of unstable systems by feedback, the concept of Controllability denotes the ability to move a system around in its entire configuration space using only certain admissible manipulations.
Cost	In business, retail, and accounting, a cost is the value of money that has been used up to produce something, and hence is not available for use anymore. In economics, a cost is an alternative that is given up as a result of a decision. In business, the cost may be one of acquisition, in which case the amount of money expended to acquire it is counted as cost.
Transaction cost	In economics and related disciplines, a Transaction cost is a cost incurred in making an economic exchange (restated: the cost of participating in a market). For example, most people, when buying or selling a stock, must pay a commission to their broker; that commission is a Transaction cost of doing the stock deal. Or consider buying a banana from a store; to purchase the banana, your costs will be not only the price of the banana itself, but also the energy and effort it requires to find out which of the various banana products you prefer, where to get them and at what price, the cost of traveling from your house to the store and back, the time waiting in line, and the effort of the paying itself; the costs above and beyond the cost of the banana are the Transaction costs.
Ex-ante	The term ex-ante is a neo-Latin word meaning "before the event". ex-ante is used most commonly in the commercial world, where results of a particular action, or series of actions, are forecast in advance. The opposite of ex-ante is ex-post (or ex post).
Hypothesis	A hypothesis is a proposed explanation for an observable phenomenon. The term derives from the Greek, hypotithenai meaning "to put under" or "to suppose." For a hypothesis to be put forward as a scientific hypothesis, the scientific method requires that one can test it. Scientists generally base scientific hypotheses on previous observations that cannot be satisfactorily explained with the available scientific theories.
Markets	A market is any one of a variety of different systems, institutions, procedures, social relations and infrastructures whereby persons trade, and goods and services are exchanged, forming part of the economy. It is an arrangement that allows buyers and sellers to exchange things. markets vary in size, range, geographic scale, location, types and variety of human communities, as well as the types of goods and services traded.

Chapter 6. AN ECONOMIC THEORY OF CONTRACT

Chapter 6. AN ECONOMIC THEORY OF CONTRACT

Market failure	In economics, a Market failure exists when the production or use of goods and services by the market is not efficient. That is, there exists another outcome where market participants" total gains from the new outcome outweigh their losses (even if some participants lose under the new arrangement). Market failures can be viewed as scenarios where individuals" pursuit of pure self-interest leads to results that are not efficient - that can be improved upon from the societal point-of-view.
Regulation	Regulation refers to "controlling human or societal behaviour by rules or restrictions." Regulation can take many forms: legal restrictions promulgated by a government authority, self-Regulation, social Regulation (e.g. norms), co-Regulation and market Regulation. One can consider Regulation as actions of conduct imposing sanctions (such as a fine). This action of administrative law, or implementing regulatory law, may be contrasted with statutory or case law.
Rationality	In philosophy, Rationality and reason are the key methods used to analyze the data gathered through systematically gathered observations. In economics, sociology, and political science, a decision or situation is often called rational if it is in some sense optimal, and individuals or organizations are often called rational if they tend to act somehow optimally in pursuit of their goals. Thus one speaks, for example, of a rational allocation of resources, or of a rational corporate strategy.
Externality	In economics, an Externality or spillover of an economic transaction is an impact on a party that is not directly involved in the transaction. In such a case, prices do not reflect the full costs or benefits in production or consumption of a product or service. An advantageous impact is called an external benefit or positive Externality, while a detrimental impact is called an external cost or negative Externality.
Macro derivative	A macro derivative or an economic derivative is a derivative that is based on a macroeconomic figure, such as consumer confidence, jobless claims, in 2002 Goldman Sachs and Deutsche Bank announced to offer their clients auctions for derivatives based on macroeconomic key figures. In 2005 Deutsche Bank left the joint project.
Cartel	A Cartel is a formal (explicit) agreement among firms. It is a formal organization of producers that agree to coordinate prices and production. Cartels usually occur in an oligopolistic industry, where there is a small number of sellers and usually involve homogeneous products.
External	In economics, an externality or spillover of an economic transaction is an impact on a party that is not directly involved in the transaction. In such a case, prices do not reflect the full costs or benefits in production or consumption of a product or service. An advantageous impact is called an external benefit or positive externality, while a detrimental impact is called an external cost or negative externality.
External cost	In economics, an externality or spillover of an economic transaction is an impact on a party that is not directly involved in the transaction. In such a case, prices do not reflect the full costs or benefits in production or consumption of a product or service. An advantageous impact is called an external benefit or positive externality, while a detrimental impact is called an external cost or negative externality.

Chapter 6. AN ECONOMIC THEORY OF CONTRACT

Chapter 6. AN ECONOMIC THEORY OF CONTRACT

Liability	In financial accounting, a Liability is defined as an obligation of an entity arising from past transactions or events, the settlement of which may result in the transfer or use of assets, provision of services or other yielding of economic benefits in the future.

· All type of borrowing from persons or banks for improving a business or person income which is payable during short or long time.
· They embody a duty or responsibility to others that entails settlement by future transfer or use of assets, provision of services or other yielding of economic benefits, at a specified or determinable date, on occurrence of a specified event, or on demand;
· The duty or responsibility obligates the entity leaving it little or no discretion to avoid it; and,
· The transaction or event obligating the entity has already occurred.
Liabilities in financial accounting need not be legally enforceable; but can be based on equitable obligations or constructive obligations. An equitable obligation is a duty based on ethical or moral considerations. |
Statute	A statute is a formal written enactment of a legislative authority that governs a country, state, city, or county. Typically, statutes command or prohibit something, or declare policy. The word is often used to distinguish law made by legislative bodies from case law and the regulations issued by Government agencies.
Duty	Duty (from "due," that which is owing, O. Fr. deu, did, past participle of devoir; Lat. debere, debitum; cf.
Good	In macroeconomics and accounting, a good is contrasted with a service. In this sense, a good is defined as a physical (tangible) product, capable of being delivered to a purchaser and involves the transfer of ownership from seller to customer, say an apple, as opposed to an (intangible) service, say a haircut. A more general term that preserves the distinction between goods and services is "commodities," like a flashlight.
Good faith	Good faith, is the mental and moral state of honesty, conviction as to the truth or falsehood of a proposition or body of opinion, or as to the rectitude or depravity of a line of conduct. This concept is important in law, especially equitable matters.
In contemporary English, "bona fides" is sometimes used as a synonym for credentials, background, or documentation of a person"s identity.
Fraud	In the broadest sense, a Fraud is an intentional deception made for personal gain or to damage another individual. The specific legal definition varies by legal jurisdiction. Fraud is a crime, and is also a civil law violation.
Monopoly	In economics, a Monopoly exists when a specific individual or an enterprise has sufficient control over a particular product or service to determine significantly the terms on which other individuals shall have access to it. Monopolies are thus characterized by a lack of economic competition for the good or service that they provide and a lack of viable substitute goods. The verb "monopolize" refers to the process by which a firm gains persistently greater market share than what is expected under perfect competition.

Chapter 6. AN ECONOMIC THEORY OF CONTRACT

Chapter 6. AN ECONOMIC THEORY OF CONTRACT

Monopolies	In economics, a monopoly exists when a specific individual or an enterprise has sufficient control over a particular product or service to determine significantly the terms on which other individuals shall have access to it. monopolies are thus characterized by a lack of economic competition for the good or service that they provide and a lack of viable substitute goods. The verb "monopolize" refers to the process by which a firm gains persistently greater market share than what is expected under perfect competition.
Coase Theorem	In law and economics, the Coase theorem, attributed to Ronald Coase, describes the economic efficiency of an economic allocation or outcome in the presence of externalities. The theorem states that when trade in an externality is possible and there are no transaction costs, bargaining will lead to an efficient outcome regardless of the initial allocation of property rights. In practice, obstacles to bargaining or poorly defined property rights can prevent Coasian bargaining.
Long-run	In economic models, the long-run time frame assumes no fixed factors of production. Firms can enter or leave the marketplace, and the cost (and availability) of land, labor, raw materials, and capital goods can be assumed to vary. In contrast, in the short-run time frame, certain factors are assumed to be fixed, because there is not sufficient time for them to change.
Trade	Trade is the voluntary exchange of goods, services, or both. Trade is also called commerce or transaction. A mechanism that allows Trade is called a market.
Debt compliance	In finance, the term Debt compliance describes various legal measures taken to ensure that debtors, whether individuals, businesses, honor their debts and make an honest effort to repay the money that they owe. Generally regarded as a subdivision of tax law, Debt compliance is most often enforced through a combination of audits and legal restrictions. For example, a provision of the Federal Debt Collection Procedure Act states that a person or organization indebted to the United States, against whom a judgment lien has been filed, is ineligible to receive a government grant.
Production	Production refers to the economic process of converting of inputs into outputs and is a field of study in microeconomics. Production uses resources to create a good or service that is suitable for exchange. This can include manufacturing, storing, shipping, and packaging.
Appropriation	Appropriation is the act of taking possession of or assigning purpose to properties or ideas and is important in many topics, including: · Appropriation (sociology) in relation to the spread of knowledge · Appropriation (art)

Chapter 6. AN ECONOMIC THEORY OF CONTRACT

Chapter 6. AN ECONOMIC THEORY OF CONTRACT

· Appropriation (music) in reference to the re-use and proliferation of different types of music
· Appropriation (economics) origination of human ownership of previously unowned natural resources such as land
· Appropriation (law) as a component of government spending
· Cultural Appropriation is the borrowing, or theft, of an element of cultural expression of one group by another.
· The tort of Appropriation is one form of invasion of privacy
· Appropriation (By Any Other Name) "

Trial

In law, a trial is when parties come together to a dispute present information (in the form of evidence) in a formal setting, usually a court, before a judge, jury, in order to achieve a resolution to their dispute.

· Where the trial is held before a group of members of the community, it is called a jury trial.
· Where the trial is held solely before a judge, it is called a bench trial. Bench trials involve fewer formalities, and are typically resolved faster. Furthermore, a favorable ruling for one party in a bench trial will frequently lead the other party to offer a settlement.

Valuation

In finance, valuation is the process of estimating the potential market value of a financial asset or liability. valuations can be done on assets (for example, investments in marketable securities such as stocks, options, business enterprises, or intangible assets such as patents and trademarks) or on liabilities (e.g., Bonds issued by a company). valuations are required in many contexts including investment analysis, capital budgeting, merger and acquisition transactions, financial reporting, taxable events to determine the proper tax liability, and in litigation.
valuation of financial assets is done using one or more of these types of models:

· Discounted Cash Flows determine the value by estimating the expected future earnings from owning the asset discounted to their present value.
· Relative value models determine the value based on the market prices of similar assets.
· Option pricing models are used for certain types of financial assets (e.g., warrants, put options, call options, employee stock options, investments with embedded options such as a callable bond) and are a complex present value model.

Chapter 6. AN ECONOMIC THEORY OF CONTRACT

Chapter 7. TOPICS IN THE ECONOMICS OF CONTRACT LAW

Breach of contract	Breach of contract is a legal concept in which a binding agreement or bargained-for exchange is not honored by one or more of the parties to the contract by non-performance or interference with the other party"s performance. A minor breach, a partial breach or an immaterial breach, occurs when the non-breaching party is unentitled to an order for performance of its obligations, but only to collect the actual amount of their damages. For example, suppose a homeowner hires a contractor to install new plumbing and insists that the pipes, which will ultimately be sealed behind the walls, be red.
Code	In communications, a Code is a rule for converting a piece of information (for example, a letter, word, phrase) into another form or representation (one sign into another sign), not necessarily of the same type. In communications and information processing, encoding is the process by which information from a source is converted into symbols to be communicated. Decoding is the reverse process, converting these Code symbols back into information understandable by a receiver.
Mercantile	Mercantile (or Commercial) Agencies, is the name given in United States to organizations designed to collect, record and distribute to regular clients information relative to the standing of commercial firms. In Great Britain and some European countries trade protective societies, composed of merchants and tradesmen, are formed for the promotion of trade, and members exchange information regarding the standing of business houses. These societies had their origin in the associations formed in the middle of the 18th century for the purpose of disseminating information regarding bankruptcies, assignments and bills of sale.
Damages	In law, Damages are money claimed by or ordered to be paid to a person as compensation for loss or injury. Compensatory Damages, also called actual Damages, are paid to compensate the claimant for loss, injury, or harm suffered by another"s breach of duty. On a breach of contract by a defendant, a court generally awards the sum that would restore the injured party to the economic position they expected from performance of the promise or promises (known as an "expectation measure" or "benefit-of-the-bargain" measure of Damages).
Elawyering	The term Elawyering or e-lawyering is a neologism used to refer to the practice of law over the Internet, in a way more expansive than a mere legal related internet advertisement for a service, lawyer, Elawyering initiatives have been undertaken by the American Bar Association in order to reach a "latent market" of lower and middle class citizens in need of legal services. Lawyers practicing law online are also referred to as "virtual lawyers" and practice from virtual law offices.
Restatement	The Restatements of the Law are treatises on U.S. legal topics published by the American Law Institute, an organization of legal academics and practitioners, as scholarly refinements of black-letter law, to "address uncertainty in the law through a Restatement of basic legal subjects that would tell judges and lawyers what the law was." As Harvard Law School describes the Restatements: The ALI"s aim is to distill the "black letter law" from cases, to indicate a trend in common law, and, occasionally, to recommend what a rule of law should be. In essence, they restate existing common law into a series of principles or rules.

Chapter 7. TOPICS IN THE ECONOMICS OF CONTRACT LAW

Chapter 7. TOPICS IN THE ECONOMICS OF CONTRACT LAW

	While considered secondary authority (compare to primary authority), the authoritativeness of the Restatements of the Law is evidenced by their acceptance by courts throughout the United States.
Uniform Commercial Code	The Uniform Commercial Code (Uniform Commercial Code or the Code), first published in 1952, is one of a number of uniform acts that have been promulgated in conjunction with efforts to harmonize the law of sales and other commercial transactions in all 50 states within the United States of America. This objective is deemed important because of the prevalence of commercial transactions that extend beyond one state . If the Uniform Commercial Code had not been adopted, it is likely that the Congress of the United States, exercising its authority under the Commerce Clause of the United States Constitution would have enacted national legislation. The Uniform Commercial Code therefore achieved the goal of achieving substantial uniformity in commercial legislation and, at the same time, allowed the states needed flexibility to meet local circumstances.
Contract	In common-law systems, the five key requirements for the creation of a contract are: 1. offer and acceptance (agreement) 2. consideration 3. an intention to create legal relations 4. legal capacity 5. formalities In civil-law systems, the concept of consideration is not central. In addition, for some contracts formalities must be complied with under what is sometimes called a statute of frauds. One of the most famous cases on forming a contract is Carlill v. Carbolic Smoke Ball Company, decided in nineteenth-century England.
Performance	A Performance, in performing arts, generally comprises an event in which one group of people (the performer or performers) behave in a particular way for another group of people (the audience). Sometimes the dividing line between performer and the audience may become blurred, as in the example of "participatory theatre" where audience members might get involved in the production. Singing choral music, and performing in a ballet are examples.
Expectation damages	Expectation damages are a form of damages available as a recourse to a breached contract. When a contracting party fails to fulfill their contractual duties, which causes losses to the other party, the party in breach can be liable for the losses of the other party. Losses that relate to the consequences of breach are Expectation damages, because the purpose of this type of remedy is to put the plaintiff in the position he would have been in had the contract been fulfilled.
Fraud	In the broadest sense, a Fraud is an intentional deception made for personal gain or to damage another individual. The specific legal definition varies by legal jurisdiction. Fraud is a crime, and is also a civil law violation.
Statute	A statute is a formal written enactment of a legislative authority that governs a country, state, city, or county. Typically, statutes command or prohibit something, or declare policy. The word is often used to distinguish law made by legislative bodies from case law and the regulations issued by Government agencies.
Statute of Frauds	The Statute of Frauds refers to the requirement that certain kinds of contracts be memorialized in a signed writing.

Chapter 7. TOPICS IN THE ECONOMICS OF CONTRACT LAW

Chapter 7. TOPICS IN THE ECONOMICS OF CONTRACT LAW

Traditionally, the Statute of Frauds requires a writing signed by the defendant in the following circumstances:

· Contracts in consideration of marriage.
· Contracts which cannot be performed within one year.
· Contracts for the transfer of an interest in land.
· Contracts by the executor of a will to pay a debt of the estate with their own money.
· Contracts for the sale of goods above a certain value.
· Contracts in which one party becomes a surety (acts as guarantor) for another party"s debt or other obligation.

This can be remembered by the mnemonic "MY LEGS": Marriage, one year, land, executor, goods, surety.

The term Statute of Frauds comes from an English Act of Parliament passed in 1677 (authored by Sir Leoline Jenkins and passed by the Cavalier Parliament), and more properly called An Act for Prevention of Frauds and Perjuries.

Opportunity cost

Opportunity cost or economic opportunity loss is the value of the next best alternative forgone as the result of making a decision. Opportunity cost analysis is an important part of a company"s decision-making processes but is not treated as an actual cost in any financial statement. The next best thing that a person can engage in is referred to as the Opportunity cost of doing the best thing and ignoring the next best thing to be done.

Consumer

Consumer is a broad label that refers to any individuals or households that use goods and services generated within the economy. The concept of a Consumer is used in different contexts, so that the usage and significance of the term may vary.

Typically when business people and economists talk of Consumers they are talking about person as Consumer, an aggregated commodity item with little individuality other than that expressed in the buy/not-buy decision.

Performance bond

A Performance bond is a surety bond issued by an insurance company or a bank to guarantee satisfactory completion of a project by a contractor.

For example, a contractor may cause a Performance bond to be issued in favor of a client for whom the contractor is constructing a building. If the contractor fails to construct the building according to the specifications laid out by the contract (most often due to the bankruptcy of the contractor), the client is guaranteed compensation for any monetary loss up to the amount of the Performance bond.

Chief brand officer

A Chief brand officer is a relatively new executive level position at a corporation, company, organization, typically reporting directly to the CEO or board of directors. The Chief brand officer is responsible for a brand"s image, experience, and promise, and propagating it throughout all aspects of the company. The brand officer oversees marketing, advertising, design, public relations and customer service departments. The brand equity of a company is seen as becoming increasingly dependent on the role of a Chief brand officer.

Companies that currently employ a Chief brand officer include:

Chapter 7. TOPICS IN THE ECONOMICS OF CONTRACT LAW

Chapter 7. TOPICS IN THE ECONOMICS OF CONTRACT LAW

- Srinivas Kumar, Baskin-Robbins Worldwide
- Michael Keller, Dairy Queen
- Will Kussell, Dunkin" Brands, Inc.
- Trey Hall, Boston Market Corporation
- Allen Schiffenbaure, G 2 Marketing Group
- Alan Bergstrom, Storyminers Inc.
- Brian Igoe, Metabolix, Inc.
- Phil Mcaveety, Luxury Collection
- Mark I. McCallum, Brown-Forman Corporation
- Phil McAveety, Starwood Hotels ' Resorts Worldwide, Inc.
- Danny Meisenheimer, Souper Salad, Inc

Cooperation	Distinguish from Corporation. Cooperation, co-operation, or coöperation is the process of working or acting together, which can be accomplished by both intentional and non-intentional agents. In its simplest form it involves things working in harmony, side by side, while in its more complicated forms, it can involve something as complex as the inner workings of a human being or even the social patterns of a nation.
Price	Price in economics and business is the result of an exchange and from that trade we assign a numerical monetary value to a good, service or asset. If Alice trades Bob 4 apples for an orange, the price of an orange is 4 apples. Inversely, the price of an apple is 1/4 oranges.
Investment	Investment or investing is a term with several closely-related meanings in business management, finance and economics, related to saving or deferring consumption. Investing is the active redirection of resources: from being consumed today, to creating benefits in the future; the use of assets to earn income or profit. An Investment is a choice by an individual or an organization such as a pension fund, after at least some careful analysis or thought, to place or lend money in a vehicle (e.g. property, stock securities, bonds) that has sufficiently low risk and provides the possibility of generating returns over a period of time.
Limitations	A statute of limitations is a statute in a common law legal system that sets forth the maximum period of time, after certain events, that legal proceedings based on those events may be initiated. In civil law systems, similar provisions are usually part of the civil code or criminal code and are often known collectively as "periods of prescription" or "prescriptive periods." Common law legal system might have a statute limiting the time for prosecution of crimes called misdemeanors to two years after the offense occurred. In that statute, if a person is discovered to have committed a misdemeanor three years ago, the time has expired for the prosecution of the misdemeanor.
Incentive	In economics and sociology, an Incentive is any factor (financial or non-financial) that enables or motivates a particular course of action, the study of Incentive structures is central to the study of all economic activity (both in terms of individual decision-making and in terms of co-operation and competition within a larger institutional structure).

Chapter 7. TOPICS IN THE ECONOMICS OF CONTRACT LAW

Chapter 7. TOPICS IN THE ECONOMICS OF CONTRACT LAW

Liability	In financial accounting, a Liability is defined as an obligation of an entity arising from past transactions or events, the settlement of which may result in the transfer or use of assets, provision of services or other yielding of economic benefits in the future. · All type of borrowing from persons or banks for improving a business or person income which is payable during short or long time. · They embody a duty or responsibility to others that entails settlement by future transfer or use of assets, provision of services or other yielding of economic benefits, at a specified or determinable date, on occurrence of a specified event, or on demand; · The duty or responsibility obligates the entity leaving it little or no discretion to avoid it; and, · The transaction or event obligating the entity has already occurred. Liabilities in financial accounting need not be legally enforceable; but can be based on equitable obligations or constructive obligations. An equitable obligation is a duty based on ethical or moral considerations.
Solution	In chemistry, a Solution is a homogeneous mixture composed of two or more substances. In such a mixture, a solute is dissolved in another substance, known as a solvent. Gases may dissolve in liquids, for example, carbon dioxide or oxygen in water.
Hypothesis	A hypothesis is a proposed explanation for an observable phenomenon. The term derives from the Greek, hypotithenai meaning "to put under" or "to suppose." For a hypothesis to be put forward as a scientific hypothesis, the scientific method requires that one can test it. Scientists generally base scientific hypotheses on previous observations that cannot be satisfactorily explained with the available scientific theories.
Marginal cost	In economics and finance, Marginal cost is the change in total cost that arises when the quantity produced changes by one unit. It is the cost of producing one more unit of a good. Mathematically, the Marginal cost function is expressed as the first derivative of the total cost (TC) function with respect to quantity (Q).
Future	Futures may mean: · Futures contract, a tradable financial contract · Futures exchange, a financial market where Futures contracts are traded · Futures (magazine), an American finance magazine · Futures studies, multidisciplinary studies of patterns to determine the likelihood of Future trends · Futures (journal), an international Futures studies journal · Futures (album), a 2004 release by Jimmy Eat World · "Futures" (song), a single from the above album

Chapter 7. TOPICS IN THE ECONOMICS OF CONTRACT LAW

Chapter 7. TOPICS IN THE ECONOMICS OF CONTRACT LAW

	· Futures and promises, computer programming objects that act as proxies for results that are not yet determined · Futures tournaments, minor professional tennis events .
Futures contract	Futures contract, in finance, refers to a standardized contract to buy or sell a specified commodity of standardized quality at a certain date in the future, at a market determined price (the futures price). The contracts are traded on a futures exchange. futures contracts are not "direct" securities like stocks, bonds, rights or warrants as outlined by the Uniform Securities Act.
Regulatory	Regulation refers to "controlling human or societal behaviour by rules or restrictions." Regulation can take many forms: legal restrictions promulgated by a government authority, self-regulation, social regulation (e.g. norms), co-regulation and market regulation. One can consider regulation as actions of conduct imposing sanctions (such as a fine). This action of administrative law, or implementing regulatory law, may be contrasted with statutory or case law.
Demand	In economics, demand is the desire to own anything and the ability to pay for it. . The term demand signifies the ability or the willingness to buy a particular commodity at a given point of time.
Anecdotal value	In economics, Anecdotal value refers to the primarily social and political value of an anecdote or anecdotal evidence in promoting understanding of a social, cultural, in the last several decades the evaluation of anecdotes has received sustained academic scrutiny from economists and scholars such as S.G. Checkland (on David Ricardo), Steven Novella, Hollis Robbins, R. Charleton, Kwamena Kwansah-Aidoo, and others; these academics seek to quantify the value inherent in the deployment of anecdotes. More recently, economists studying choice models have begun assessing Anecdotal value in the context of framing; Kahneman and Tversky suggest that choice models may be contingent on stories or anecdotes that frame or influence choice.
Force majeure	Force majeure , also known as cas fortuit or casus fortuitus , is a common clause in contracts which essentially frees both parties from liability or obligation when an extraordinary event or circumstance beyond the control of the parties, such as a war, strike, riot, crime or an event described by the legal term "act of God" (e.g., flooding, earthquake, volcano), prevents one or both parties from fulfilling their obligations under the contract. However, Force majeure is not intended to excuse negligence or other malfeasance of a party, as where non-performance is caused by the usual and natural consequences of external forces (e.g., predicted rain stops an outdoor event) or where the intervening circumstances are specifically contemplated.
Elasticity	In economics, elasticity is the ratio of the percent change in one variable to the percent change in another variable. It is a tool for measuring the responsiveness of a function to changes in parameters in a relative way. Commonly analyzed are elasticity of substitution, price and wealth.
Inelastic demand	Perfectly inelastic demand Perfectly elastic demand

Chapter 7. TOPICS IN THE ECONOMICS OF CONTRACT LAW

Chapter 7. TOPICS IN THE ECONOMICS OF CONTRACT LAW

	A price fall usually results in an increase in the quantity demanded by consumers. The demand for a good is relatively inelastic when the change in quantity demanded is less than change in price. Goods and services for which no substitutes exist are generally inelastic.
Information	Information as a concept has many meanings, from everyday usage to technical settings. The concept of Information is closely related to notions of constraint, communication, control, data, form, instruction, knowledge, meaning, mental stimulus, pattern, perception, and representation. The English word was apparently derived from the Latin accusative form of the nominative (informatio): this noun is in its turn derived from the verb "informare" (to inform) in the sense of "to give form to the mind", "to discipline", "instruct", "teach": "Men so wise should go and inform their kings." (1330) Inform itself comes from the Latin verb informare, to give form to, to form an idea of.
Unilateralism	Unilateralism is any doctrine or agenda that supports one-sided action. Such action may be in disregard for other parties, or as an expression of a commitment toward a direction which other parties may find agreeable. Unilateralism is a neologism, (used in all countries) coined to be an antonym for multilateralism --the doctrine which asserts the benefits of participation from as many parties as possible.
Acquisition	The phrase mergers and Acquisitions refers to the aspect of corporate strategy, corporate finance and management dealing with the buying, selling and combining of different companies that can aid, finance, or help a growing company in a given industry grow rapidly without having to create another business entity. An Acquisition, also known as a takeover or a buyout, is the buying of one company (the "target") by another. An Acquisition may be friendly or hostile.
Duty	Duty (from "due," that which is owing, O. Fr. deu, did, past participle of devoir; Lat. debere, debitum; cf.
Misrepresentation	Misrepresentation is a contract law concept. It means a false statement of fact made by one party to another party, which has the effect of inducing that party into the contract. For example, under certain circumstances, false statements or promises made by a seller of goods regarding the quality or nature of the product that the seller has may constitute Misrepresentation. A finding of Misrepresentation allows for a remedy of rescission and sometimes damages depending on the type of Misrepresentation.
Monopoly	In economics, a Monopoly exists when a specific individual or an enterprise has sufficient control over a particular product or service to determine significantly the terms on which other individuals shall have access to it. Monopolies are thus characterized by a lack of economic competition for the good or service that they provide and a lack of viable substitute goods. The verb "monopolize" refers to the process by which a firm gains persistently greater market share than what is expected under perfect competition.

Chapter 7. TOPICS IN THE ECONOMICS OF CONTRACT LAW

Chapter 7. TOPICS IN THE ECONOMICS OF CONTRACT LAW

Cartel	A Cartel is a formal (explicit) agreement among firms. It is a formal organization of producers that agree to coordinate prices and production. Cartels usually occur in an oligopolistic industry, where there is a small number of sellers and usually involve homogeneous products.
Competition	Co-operative Competition is based upon promoting mutual survival - "everyone wins". Adam Smith"s "invisible hand" is a process where individuals compete to improve their level of happiness but compete in a cooperative manner through peaceful exchange and without violating other people. Cooperative Competition focuses individuals/groups/organisms against the environment.
Transaction cost	In economics and related disciplines, a Transaction cost is a cost incurred in making an economic exchange (restated: the cost of participating in a market). For example, most people, when buying or selling a stock, must pay a commission to their broker; that commission is a Transaction cost of doing the stock deal. Or consider buying a banana from a store; to purchase the banana, your costs will be not only the price of the banana itself, but also the energy and effort it requires to find out which of the various banana products you prefer, where to get them and at what price, the cost of traveling from your house to the store and back, the time waiting in line, and the effort of the paying itself; the costs above and beyond the cost of the banana are the Transaction costs.
Down payment	Down payment (or downpayment) is a term used in the context of the purchase of expensive items such as a car and a house, whereby the payment is the initial upfront portion of the total amount due and it is usually given in cash at the time of finalizing the transaction. A loan is then required to make the full payment. The main purpose of a Down payment is to ensure that the lending institution can recover the balance due on the loan in the event that the borrower defaults.
Security	A securitiy is a fungible, negotiable instrument representing financial value. Securities are broadly categorized into debt securities (such as banknotes, bonds and debentures); equity securities, e.g., common stocks; and derivative contracts, such as forwards, futures, options and swaps. The company or other entity issuing the Security is called the issuer.
Security interest	A Security interest is a property interest created by agreement or by operation of law over assets to secure the performance of an obligation, usually the payment of a debt. It gives the beneficiary of the Security interest certain preferential rights in the disposition of secured assets. Such rights vary according to the type of Security interest, but in most cases, a holder of the Security interest is entitled to seize, and usually sell, the property to discharge the debt that the Security interest secures.
Probability	Probability is a way of expressing knowledge or belief that an event will occur or has occurred. In mathematics the concept has been given an exact meaning in probability theory, that is used extensively in such areas of study as mathematics, statistics, finance, gambling, science, and philosophy to draw conclusions about the likelihood of potential events and the underlying mechanics of complex systems. The word probability does not have a consistent direct definition. In fact, there are two broad categories of probability interpretations, whose adherents possess different (and sometimes conflicting) views about the fundamental nature of probability:

Chapter 7. TOPICS IN THE ECONOMICS OF CONTRACT LAW

Chapter 7. TOPICS IN THE ECONOMICS OF CONTRACT LAW

	· Frequentists talk about probabilities only when dealing with experiments that are random and well-defined.
Coase Theorem	In law and economics, the Coase theorem, attributed to Ronald Coase, describes the economic efficiency of an economic allocation or outcome in the presence of externalities. The theorem states that when trade in an externality is possible and there are no transaction costs, bargaining will lead to an efficient outcome regardless of the initial allocation of property rights. In practice, obstacles to bargaining or poorly defined property rights can prevent Coasian bargaining.
Measure	The measures used in economics are physical measures, nominal price value measures and fixed price value measures. These measures differ from one another by the variables they measure and by the variables excluded from measurements. The measurable variables in economics are quantity, quality and distribution.
Controllability	Controllability is an important property of a control system, and the Controllability property plays a crucial role in many control problems, such as stabilization of unstable systems by feedback, the concept of Controllability denotes the ability to move a system around in its entire configuration space using only certain admissible manipulations.

Chapter 7. TOPICS IN THE ECONOMICS OF CONTRACT LAW

Chapter 8. AN ECONOMIC THEORY OF TORT LAW

Tort	Tort law is a body of law that addresses, and provides remedies for, civil wrongs not arising out of contractual obligations. A person who suffers legal damages may be able to use Tort law to receive compensation from someone who is legally responsible, or liable, for those injuries. Generally speaking, Tort law defines what constitutes a legal injury and establishes the circumstances under which one person may be held liable for another"s injury.
Elawyering	The term Elawyering or e-lawyering is a neologism used to refer to the practice of law over the Internet, in a way more expansive than a mere legal related internet advertisement for a service, lawyer, Elawyering initiatives have been undertaken by the American Bar Association in order to reach a "latent market" of lower and middle class citizens in need of legal services. Lawyers practicing law online are also referred to as "virtual lawyers" and practice from virtual law offices.
Transaction cost	In economics and related disciplines, a Transaction cost is a cost incurred in making an economic exchange (restated: the cost of participating in a market). For example, most people, when buying or selling a stock, must pay a commission to their broker; that commission is a Transaction cost of doing the stock deal. Or consider buying a banana from a store; to purchase the banana, your costs will be not only the price of the banana itself, but also the energy and effort it requires to find out which of the various banana products you prefer, where to get them and at what price, the cost of traveling from your house to the store and back, the time waiting in line, and the effort of the paying itself; the costs above and beyond the cost of the banana are the Transaction costs.
Bargaining	Bargaining or haggling is a type of negotiation in which the buyer and seller of a good or service dispute the price which will be paid and the exact nature of the transaction that will take place, and eventually come to an agreement. Bargaining is an alternative pricing strategy to fixed prices. Optimally, if it costs the retailer nothing to engage and allow Bargaining, he can divine the buyer"s willingness to spend.
Duty	Duty (from "due," that which is owing, O. Fr. deu, did, past participle of devoir; Lat. debere, debitum; cf.
Limitations	A statute of limitations is a statute in a common law legal system that sets forth the maximum period of time, after certain events, that legal proceedings based on those events may be initiated. In civil law systems, similar provisions are usually part of the civil code or criminal code and are often known collectively as "periods of prescription" or "prescriptive periods." Common law legal system might have a statute limiting the time for prosecution of crimes called misdemeanors to two years after the offense occurred. In that statute, if a person is discovered to have committed a misdemeanor three years ago, the time has expired for the prosecution of the misdemeanor.
Dot-com bubble	The "Dot-com bubble" (or) was a speculative bubble covering roughly 1998-2001 (with a climax on March 10, 2000 with the NASDAQ peaking at 5132.52) during which stock markets in Western nations saw their equity value rise rapidly from growth in the more recent Internet sector and related fields. While the latter part was a boom and bust cycle, the Internet boom sometimes is meant to refer to the steady commercial growth of the Internet with the advent of the world wide web as exemplified by the first release of the Mosaic web browser in 1993 and continuing through the 1990s.

Chapter 8. AN ECONOMIC THEORY OF TORT LAW

Chapter 8. AN ECONOMIC THEORY OF TORT LAW

	The period was marked by the founding (and, in many cases, spectacular failure) of a group of new Internet-based companies commonly referred to as dot-coms.
Liability	In financial accounting, a Liability is defined as an obligation of an entity arising from past transactions or events, the settlement of which may result in the transfer or use of assets, provision of services or other yielding of economic benefits in the future. · All type of borrowing from persons or banks for improving a business or person income which is payable during short or long time. · They embody a duty or responsibility to others that entails settlement by future transfer or use of assets, provision of services or other yielding of economic benefits, at a specified or determinable date, on occurrence of a specified event, or on demand; · The duty or responsibility obligates the entity leaving it little or no discretion to avoid it; and, · The transaction or event obligating the entity has already occurred. Liabilities in financial accounting need not be legally enforceable; but can be based on equitable obligations or constructive obligations. An equitable obligation is a duty based on ethical or moral considerations.
Negligence	Negligence is a legal concept in the common law legal systems usually used to achieve compensation for injuries (not accidents). Negligence is a type of tort or delict (also known as a civil wrong).
Anecdotal value	In economics, Anecdotal value refers to the primarily social and political value of an anecdote or anecdotal evidence in promoting understanding of a social, cultural, in the last several decades the evaluation of anecdotes has received sustained academic scrutiny from economists and scholars such as S.G. Checkland (on David Ricardo), Steven Novella, Hollis Robbins, R. Charleton, Kwamena Kwansah-Aidoo, and others; these academics seek to quantify the value inherent in the deployment of anecdotes. More recently, economists studying choice models have begun assessing Anecdotal value in the context of framing; Kahneman and Tversky suggest that choice models may be contingent on stories or anecdotes that frame or influence choice.
Code	In communications, a Code is a rule for converting a piece of information (for example, a letter, word, phrase) into another form or representation (one sign into another sign), not necessarily of the same type. In communications and information processing, encoding is the process by which information from a source is converted into symbols to be communicated. Decoding is the reverse process, converting these Code symbols back into information understandable by a receiver.
Common Law	Common law is law developed by judges through decisions of courts and similar tribunals (called case law), rather than through legislative statutes or executive action, and to corresponding legal systems that rely on precedential case law. The body of precedent is called "Common law" and it binds future decisions. In future cases, when parties disagree on what the law is, an idealized Common law court looks to past precedential decisions of relevant courts.

Chapter 8. AN ECONOMIC THEORY OF TORT LAW

Chapter 8. AN ECONOMIC THEORY OF TORT LAW

Social	The term social refers to a characteristic of living organisms (humans in particular, though biologists also apply the term to populations of other animals). It always refers to the interaction of organisms with other organisms and to their collective co-existence, irrespective of whether they are aware of it or not, and irrespective of whether the interaction is voluntary or involuntary. In the absence of agreement about its meaning, the term "ps" is used in many different senses and regarded as a [[]], referringse among other things to: · Attitudes, orientations, or behaviours which take the interests, intentions, or needs of other people into account (in contrast to anti-social behaviour);has played some role in defining the idea or the principle. For instance terms like social realism, social justice, social constructivism, social psychology and social capital imply that there is some social process involved or considered, a process that is not there in regular, "non-social", realism, justice, constructivism, psychology, or capital.
Social cost	In neoclassical economics social cost is defined as the sum of private and external costs. Neoclassical economic theorists ascribe individual decision-making to a calculation costs and benefits. Rational choice theory assumes that individuals only consider their own private costs when making decisions, not the costs that may be borne by others.
Cost-benefit	Cost-benefit analysis is a term that refers both to: · helping to appraise, or assess, the case for a project or proposal, which itself is a process known as project appraisal; and · an informal approach to making decisions of any kind. Under both definitions the process involves, whether explicitly or implicitly, weighing the total expected costs against the total expected benefits of one or more actions in order to choose the best or most profitable option. The formal process is often referred to as either CBA (cost-benefit Analysis) or BCA (Benefit-Cost Analysis).
Incentive	In economics and sociology, an Incentive is any factor (financial or non-financial) that enables or motivates a particular course of action, the study of Incentive structures is central to the study of all economic activity (both in terms of individual decision-making and in terms of co-operation and competition within a larger institutional structure).
Unilateralism	Unilateralism is any doctrine or agenda that supports one-sided action. Such action may be in disregard for other parties, or as an expression of a commitment toward a direction which other parties may find agreeable. Unilateralism is a neologism, (used in all countries) coined to be an antonym for multilateralism --the doctrine which asserts the benefits of participation from as many parties as possible.

Chapter 8. AN ECONOMIC THEORY OF TORT LAW

Chapter 8. AN ECONOMIC THEORY OF TORT LAW

Monopoly	In economics, a Monopoly exists when a specific individual or an enterprise has sufficient control over a particular product or service to determine significantly the terms on which other individuals shall have access to it. Monopolies are thus characterized by a lack of economic competition for the good or service that they provide and a lack of viable substitute goods. The verb "monopolize" refers to the process by which a firm gains persistently greater market share than what is expected under perfect competition.
Contributory negligence	Contributory negligence is a common law defense to a claim based on negligence, an action in tort. It applies to cases where a plaintiff has, through his own negligence, contributed to the harm he suffered. For example, a pedestrian crosses a road negligently and is hit by a driver who was driving negligently.
Comparative negligence	Comparative negligence, is a partial legal defense that reduces the amount of damages that a plaintiff can recover in a negligence-based claim based upon the degree to which the plaintiff's own negligence contributed to cause the injury. When the defense is asserted, the fact-finder, usually a jury, must decide the degree to which the plaintiff's negligence versus the combined negligence of all other relevant actors contributed to cause the plaintiff's damages. It is a modification of the doctrine of contributory negligence which disallows any recovery by a plaintiff whose negligence contributed, even minimally, to causing the damages.
Cost-benefit analysis	Cost-benefit analysis is a term that refers both to: · helping to appraise, or assess, the case for a project or proposal, which itself is a process known as project appraisal; and · an informal approach to making decisions of any kind. Under both definitions the process involves, whether explicitly or implicitly, weighing the total expected costs against the total expected benefits of one or more actions in order to choose the best or most profitable option. The formal process is often referred to as either CBA (Cost-benefit analysis) or BCA (Benefit-Cost Analysis).
Best practice	A Best practice is a technique, method, process, activity, incentive or reward that is believed to be more effective at delivering a particular outcome than any other technique, method, process, etc. The idea is that with proper processes, checks, and testing, a desired outcome can be delivered with fewer problems and unforeseen complications. Best practices can also be defined as the most efficient (least amount of effort) and effective (best results) way of accomplishing a task, based on repeatable procedures that have proven themselves over time for large numbers of people.
Damages	In law, Damages are money claimed by or ordered to be paid to a person as compensation for loss or injury. Compensatory Damages, also called actual Damages, are paid to compensate the claimant for loss, injury, or harm suffered by another"s breach of duty.

Chapter 8. AN ECONOMIC THEORY OF TORT LAW

Chapter 8. AN ECONOMIC THEORY OF TORT LAW

	On a breach of contract by a defendant, a court generally awards the sum that would restore the injured party to the economic position they expected from performance of the promise or promises (known as an "expectation measure" or "benefit-of-the-bargain" measure of Damages).
Calendar	A Calendar is a system of organizing days for social, religious, commercial, typically days, weeks, months, and years. The name given to each day is known as a date.
Supreme Court	A Supreme Court (, court of final appeal or high court) is in some jurisdictions the highest judicial body within that jurisdiction"s court system, whose rulings are not subject to further review by another court. The designations for such courts differ among jurisdictions. Courts of last resort typically function primarily as appellate courts, hearing appeals from the lower trial courts or intermediate-level appellate courts.
Wholesale	Wholesaling, jobbing, to industrial, commercial, institutional, or other professional business users, or to other wholesalers and related subordinated services. According to the United Nations Statistics Division, "wholesale" is the resale (sale without transformation) of new and used goods to retailers, to industrial, commercial, institutional or professional users, or to other wholesalers, or involves acting as an agent or broker in buying merchandise for, or selling merchandise to, such persons or companies. wholesalers frequently physically assemble, sort and grade goods in large lots, break bulk, repack and redistribute in smaller lots.
Consumer	Consumer is a broad label that refers to any individuals or households that use goods and services generated within the economy. The concept of a Consumer is used in different contexts, so that the usage and significance of the term may vary. Typically when business people and economists talk of Consumers they are talking about person as Consumer, an aggregated commodity item with little individuality other than that expressed in the buy/not-buy decision.

Chapter 8. AN ECONOMIC THEORY OF TORT LAW

Chapter 9. TOPICS IN THE ECONOMICS OF TORT LIABILITY

Unilateralism	Unilateralism is any doctrine or agenda that supports one-sided action. Such action may be in disregard for other parties, or as an expression of a commitment toward a direction which other parties may find agreeable. Unilateralism is a neologism, (used in all countries) coined to be an antonym for multilateralism --the doctrine which asserts the benefits of participation from as many parties as possible.
Negligence	Negligence is a legal concept in the common law legal systems usually used to achieve compensation for injuries (not accidents). Negligence is a type of tort or delict (also known as a civil wrong).
Liability	In financial accounting, a Liability is defined as an obligation of an entity arising from past transactions or events, the settlement of which may result in the transfer or use of assets, provision of services or other yielding of economic benefits in the future. · All type of borrowing from persons or banks for improving a business or person income which is payable during short or long time. · They embody a duty or responsibility to others that entails settlement by future transfer or use of assets, provision of services or other yielding of economic benefits, at a specified or determinable date, on occurrence of a specified event, or on demand; · The duty or responsibility obligates the entity leaving it little or no discretion to avoid it; and, · The transaction or event obligating the entity has already occurred. Liabilities in financial accounting need not be legally enforceable; but can be based on equitable obligations or constructive obligations. An equitable obligation is a duty based on ethical or moral considerations.
Occupational safety and health	Occupational safety and health is a cross-disciplinary area concerned with protecting the safety, health and welfare of people engaged in work or employment. The goal of all Occupational safety and health programs is to foster a safe work environment. As a secondary effect, it may also protect co-workers, family members, employers, customers, suppliers, nearby communities, and other members of the public who are impacted by the workplace environment.
Regulation	Regulation refers to "controlling human or societal behaviour by rules or restrictions." Regulation can take many forms: legal restrictions promulgated by a government authority, self-Regulation, social Regulation (e.g. norms), co-Regulation and market Regulation. One can consider Regulation as actions of conduct imposing sanctions (such as a fine). This action of administrative law, or implementing regulatory law, may be contrasted with statutory or case law.
Calendar	A Calendar is a system of organizing days for social, religious, commercial, typically days, weeks, months, and years. The name given to each day is known as a date.
Cost	In business, retail, and accounting, a cost is the value of money that has been used up to produce something, and hence is not available for use anymore. In economics, a cost is an alternative that is given up as a result of a decision. In business, the cost may be one of acquisition, in which case the amount of money expended to acquire it is counted as cost.

Chapter 9. TOPICS IN THE ECONOMICS OF TORT LIABILITY

Chapter 9. TOPICS IN THE ECONOMICS OF TORT LIABILITY

Insurance	Insurance, in law and economics, is a form of risk management primarily used to hedge against the risk of a contingent loss. Insurance is defined as the equitable transfer of the risk of a loss, from one entity to another, in exchange for a premium, and can be thought of as a guaranteed and known small loss to prevent a large, possibly devastating loss. An insurer is a company selling the Insurance; an insured or policyholder is the person or entity buying the Insurance.
Liability insurance	Liability insurance is a part of the general insurance system of risk financing. Originally, individuals or companies that faced a common peril, formed a group and created a self-help fund out of which to pay compensation should any member incur loss. The modern system relies on dedicated carriers to offer protection against specified perils in consideration of a premium.
Subrogation	Subrogation is the legal technique under common law by which one party, commonly an insurer (I-X) of another party (X), steps into X"s shoes, so as to have the benefit of X"s rights and remedies against a third party such as a defendant (D). subrogation is similar in effect to assignment, but unlike assignment, subrogation can occur without any agreement between I-X and X to transfer X"s rights. subrogation most commonly arises in relation to policies of insurance, but the legal technique is of more general application.
Contract	In common-law systems, the five key requirements for the creation of a contract are: 1. offer and acceptance (agreement) 2. consideration 3. an intention to create legal relations 4. legal capacity 5. formalities In civil-law systems, the concept of consideration is not central. In addition, for some contracts formalities must be complied with under what is sometimes called a statute of frauds. One of the most famous cases on forming a contract is Carlill v. Carbolic Smoke Ball Company, decided in nineteenth-century England.
Ex-ante	The term ex-ante is a neo-Latin word meaning "before the event". ex-ante is used most commonly in the commercial world, where results of a particular action, or series of actions, are forecast in advance. The opposite of ex-ante is ex-post (or ex post).
Moral hazard	Moral hazard is the fact that a party insulated from risk may behave differently from the way it would behave if it would be fully exposed to the risk. In insurance, Moral hazard that occurs without conscious or malicious action is called morale hazard. Moral hazard is a special case of information asymmetry, a situation in which one party in a transaction has more information than another.
Characteristic	Characteristic has several particular meanings: · in mathematics.

Chapter 9. TOPICS IN THE ECONOMICS OF TORT LIABILITY

Chapter 9. TOPICS IN THE ECONOMICS OF TORT LIABILITY

- characteristic function
- Euler characteristic
- characteristic (algebra)
- characteristic subgroup
- method of characteristics (partial differential equations)
- in physics and engineering

- any characteristic curve that shows the relationship between certain input- and output parameters, e.g.
- an I-V or current-voltage characteristic is the current in a circuit as a function of the applied voltage
- Receiver-Operator characteristic
- in navigation, the characteristic pattern of a lighted beacon.
- in fiction

- in Dungeons ' Dragons, characteristic is another name for ability score

Industry — An industry is the manufacturing of a good or service within a category. Although industry is a broad term for any kind of economic production, in economics and urban planning industry is a synonym for the secondary sector, which is a type of economic activity involved in the manufacturing of raw materials into goods and products.

There are four key industrial economic sectors: the primary sector, largely raw material extraction industries such as mining and farming; the secondary sector, involving refining, construction, and manufacturing; the tertiary sector, which deals with services and distribution of manufactured goods; and the quaternary sector, a relatively new type of knowledge industry focusing on technological research, design and development such as computer programming, and biochemistry.

Markets — A market is any one of a variety of different systems, institutions, procedures, social relations and infrastructures whereby persons trade, and goods and services are exchanged, forming part of the economy. It is an arrangement that allows buyers and sellers to exchange things. markets vary in size, range, geographic scale, location, types and variety of human communities, as well as the types of goods and services traded.

Adverse selection — Adverse selection, anti-selection, insurance, statistics, and risk management. It refers to a market process in which "bad" results occur when buyers and sellers have asymmetric information (i.e. access to different information): the "bad" products or customers are more likely to be selected. A bank that sets one price for all its checking account customers runs the risk of being adversely selected against by its low-balance, high-activity (and hence least profitable) customers.

Funding — Funding or financing is to provide capital (funds), which means resources, usually in form of money, for a project, a person, a business or any other private or public institutions. When a request f is made then fundraising is being attempted.

Those funds can be allocated for either short term or long term purposes.

Chapter 9. TOPICS IN THE ECONOMICS OF TORT LIABILITY

Chapter 9. TOPICS IN THE ECONOMICS OF TORT LIABILITY

Bankruptcy	Bankruptcy is a legally declared inability or impairment of ability of an individual or organization to pay its creditors. Creditors may file a Bankruptcy petition against a debtor ("involuntary Bankruptcy") in an effort to recoup a portion of what they are owed or initiate a restructuring. In the majority of cases, however, Bankruptcy is initiated by the debtor (a "voluntary Bankruptcy" that is filed by the insolvent individual or organization).
Limited liability	Limited liability is a concept whereby a person"s financial liability is limited to a fixed sum, most commonly the value of a person"s investment in a company or partnership with Limited liability. In other words, if a company with Limited liability is sued, then the plaintiffs are suing the company, not its owners or investors. A shareholder in a limited company is not personally liable for any of the debts of the company, other than for the value of his investment in that company.
Securitization	Securitization is a structured finance process that distributes risk by aggregating debt instruments in a pool, then issues new securities backed by the pool. The term "Securitization" is derived from the fact that the form of financial instruments used to obtain funds from the investors are securities. As a portfolio risk backed by amortizing cash flows - and unlike general corporate debt - the credit quality of securitized debt is non-stationary due to changes in volatility that are time- and structure-dependent.
Vicarious liability	Vicarious liability is a form of strict, secondary liability that arises under the common law doctrine of agency - respondeat superior - the responsibility of the superior for the acts of their subordinate, or, in a broader sense, the responsibility of any third party that had the "right, ability or duty to control" the activities of a violator. It can be distinguished from contributory liability, another form of secondary liability, which is rooted in the tort theory of enterprise liability. Employers are vicariously liable, under the respondeat superior doctrine, for negligent acts or omissions by their employees in the course of employment.
Elawyering	The term Elawyering or e-lawyering is a neologism used to refer to the practice of law over the Internet, in a way more expansive than a mere legal related internet advertisement for a service, lawyer, Elawyering initiatives have been undertaken by the American Bar Association in order to reach a "latent market" of lower and middle class citizens in need of legal services. Lawyers practicing law online are also referred to as "virtual lawyers" and practice from virtual law offices.
Deep pocket	Deep pocket is an American slang term; it usually means "extensive financial wealth or resources". It is usually used in reference to big companies or organizations (ex: the American tobacco companies have "Deep pockets"), although it can be used in reference to individuals (e.g., Bill Gates, Donald Trump). In the context of a lawsuit, the Deep pocket is often the target defendant, even when the true (moral) culpability is with another party because the Deep pocket has money to pay a verdict.

Chapter 9. TOPICS IN THE ECONOMICS OF TORT LIABILITY

Chapter 9. TOPICS IN THE ECONOMICS OF TORT LIABILITY

Anecdotal value	In economics, Anecdotal value refers to the primarily social and political value of an anecdote or anecdotal evidence in promoting understanding of a social, cultural, in the last several decades the evaluation of anecdotes has received sustained academic scrutiny from economists and scholars such as S.G. Checkland (on David Ricardo), Steven Novella, Hollis Robbins, R. Charleton, Kwamena Kwansah-Aidoo, and others; these academics seek to quantify the value inherent in the deployment of anecdotes. More recently, economists studying choice models have begun assessing Anecdotal value in the context of framing; Kahneman and Tversky suggest that choice models may be contingent on stories or anecdotes that frame or influence choice.
Comparative negligence	Comparative negligence, is a partial legal defense that reduces the amount of damages that a plaintiff can recover in a negligence-based claim based upon the degree to which the plaintiff's own negligence contributed to cause the injury. When the defense is asserted, the fact-finder, usually a jury, must decide the degree to which the plaintiff's negligence versus the combined negligence of all other relevant actors contributed to cause the plaintiff's damages. It is a modification of the doctrine of contributory negligence which disallows any recovery by a plaintiff whose negligence contributed, even minimally, to causing the damages.
Smoothing	In statistics and image processing, Smoothing a data set is to create an approximating function that attempts to capture important patterns in the data, while leaving out noise or other fine-scale structures/rapid phenomena. Many different algorithms are used in Smoothing. One of the most common algorithms is the "moving average", often used to try to capture important trends in repeated statistical surveys.
Criticism	This article is about criticism of, and arguments against debt. There are many arguments against debt as an instrument and institution, on a personal, family, social, corporate and governmental level. Usually these refer to conditions under which debt should not be used as a solution, e.g. to fund consumption for survival.
Incentive	In economics and sociology, an Incentive is any factor (financial or non-financial) that enables or motivates a particular course of action, the study of Incentive structures is central to the study of all economic activity (both in terms of individual decision-making and in terms of co-operation and competition within a larger institutional structure).
Intellectual Property	Intellectual property is a number of distinct types of legal monopolies over creations of the mind, both artistic and commercial, and the corresponding fields of law. Under Intellectual property law, owners are granted certain exclusive rights to a variety of intangible assets, such as musical, literary, and artistic works; ideas, discoveries and inventions; and words, phrases, symbols, and designs. Common types of Intellectual property include copyrights, trademarks, patents, industrial design rights and trade secrets in some jurisdictions.
Tax	To Tax is to impose a financial charge or other levy upon a Taxpayer (an individual or legal entity) by a state or the functional equivalent of a state such that failure to pay is punishable by law.

Chapter 9. TOPICS IN THE ECONOMICS OF TORT LIABILITY

Chapter 9. TOPICS IN THE ECONOMICS OF TORT LIABILITY

	Taxes are also imposed by many subnational entities. Taxes consist of direct Tax or indirect Tax, and may be paid in money or as its labour equivalent (often but not always unpaid).
Trade	Trade is the voluntary exchange of goods, services, or both. Trade is also called commerce or transaction. A mechanism that allows Trade is called a market.
Damages	In law, Damages are money claimed by or ordered to be paid to a person as compensation for loss or injury. Compensatory Damages, also called actual Damages, are paid to compensate the claimant for loss, injury, or harm suffered by another"s breach of duty. On a breach of contract by a defendant, a court generally awards the sum that would restore the injured party to the economic position they expected from performance of the promise or promises (known as an "expectation measure" or "benefit-of-the-bargain" measure of Damages).
Tort	Tort law is a body of law that addresses, and provides remedies for, civil wrongs not arising out of contractual obligations. A person who suffers legal damages may be able to use Tort law to receive compensation from someone who is legally responsible, or liable, for those injuries. Generally speaking, Tort law defines what constitutes a legal injury and establishes the circumstances under which one person may be held liable for another"s injury.
Life	Life (cf. biota) is a characteristic that distinguishes objects that have self-sustaining biological processes from those that do not --either because such functions have ceased (death), or else because they lack such functions and are classified as "inanimate." In biology, the science of living organisms, "Life" is the condition which distinguishes active organisms from inorganic matter, including the capacity for growth, functional activity and the continual change preceding death. A diverse array of living organisms (Life forms) can be found in the biosphere on Earth, and properties common to these organisms--plants, animals, fungi, protists, archaea, and bacteria -- are a carbon- and water-based cellular form with complex organization and heritable genetic information.
Organization	Management is interested in Organization mainly from an instrumental point of view. For a company, Organization is a means to an end to achieve its goals. Among the theories that are or have been most influential are: · Pyramids or hierarchies · Committees or juries · Matrix Organizations · Ecologies A hierarchy exemplifies an arrangement with a leader who leads leaders. This arrangement is often associated with bureaucracy.

Chapter 9. TOPICS IN THE ECONOMICS OF TORT LIABILITY

Chapter 9. TOPICS IN THE ECONOMICS OF TORT LIABILITY

Trust	In common law legal systems, a Trust is an arrangement whereby property (including real, tangible and intangible) is managed by one person (or persons) for the benefit of another. A Trust is created by a settlor (or feoffor to uses), who enTrusts some or all of his property to people of his choice (the Trustees or feoffee to uses). The Trustees hold legal title to the Trust property (or Trust corpus), but they are obliged to hold the property for the benefit of one or more individuals or organizations (the beneficiary, cestui que use, or cestui que Trust), usually specified by the settlor, who hold equitable title.
Utility	In economics, Utility is a measure of the relative satisfaction from or desirability of, consumption of various goods and services. Given this measure, one may speak meaningfully of increasing or decreasing Utility, and thereby explain economic behavior in terms of attempts to increase one"s Utility. For illustrative purposes, changes in Utility are sometimes expressed in fictional units called utils (fictional in that there is no standard scale for them).
Governance	Governance relates to decisions that define expectations, grant power
Supreme Court	A Supreme Court (, court of final appeal or high court) is in some jurisdictions the highest judicial body within that jurisdiction"s court system, whose rulings are not subject to further review by another court. The designations for such courts differ among jurisdictions. Courts of last resort typically function primarily as appellate courts, hearing appeals from the lower trial courts or intermediate-level appellate courts.
Medical malpractice	Medical malpractice is professional negligence by act or omission by a health care provider in which care provided deviates from accepted standards of practice in the medical community and causes injury or death to the patient. Standards and regulations f vary by country and jurisdiction within countries. Medical professionals are required to maintain professional liability insurance to offset the risk and costs of lawsuits based on Medical malpractice.
Nominative determinism	Nominative determinism refers to the theory that a person"s name is given an influential role in reflecting key attributes of his job, profession, but real examples are more highly prized, the more obscure the better.
Defensive medicine	Defensive medicine is the practice of diagnostic or therapeutic measures conducted primarily not to ensure the health of the patient, but as a safeguard against possible malpractice liability. Fear of litigation has been cited as the driving force behind Defensive medicine. Defensive medicine is especially common in the United States of America, with rates as high as 79% to 93% , particularly in emergency medicine, obstetrics, and other high-risk specialties.
Health	At the of the creation of the World Health Organization (WHO), in 1948, Health was defined as being "a state of complete physical, mental, and social well-being and not merely the absence of disease or infirmity".

Chapter 9. TOPICS IN THE ECONOMICS OF TORT LIABILITY

Chapter 9. TOPICS IN THE ECONOMICS OF TORT LIABILITY

This definition invited nations to expand the conceptual framework of their Health systems beyond issues related to the physical condition of individuals and their diseases, and it motivated us to focus our attention on what we now call social determinants of Health. Consequently, WHO challenged political, academic, community, and professional organizations devoted to improving or preserving Health to make the scope of their work explicit, including their rationale for allocating resources.

Health care

Health care, is the treatment and management of illness, and the preservation of health through services offered by the medical, dental, complementary and alternative medicine, pharmaceutical, clinical laboratory sciences, nursing, and allied health professions. Health care embraces all the goods and services designed to promote health, including "preventive, curative and palliative interventions, whether directed to individuals or to populations".

Before the term Health care became popular, English-speakers referred to medicine or to the health sector and spoke of the treatment and prevention of illness and disease.

Market share

Market share, in strategic management and marketing is, according to Carlton O"Neal, the percentage or proportion of the total available market or market segment that is being serviced by a company. It can be expressed as a company"s sales revenue divided by the total sales revenue available in that market. It can also be expressed as a company"s unit sales volume (in a market) divided by the total volume of units sold in that market.

Dot-com bubble

The "Dot-com bubble" (or) was a speculative bubble covering roughly 1998-2001 (with a climax on March 10, 2000 with the NASDAQ peaking at 5132.52) during which stock markets in Western nations saw their equity value rise rapidly from growth in the more recent Internet sector and related fields. While the latter part was a boom and bust cycle, the Internet boom sometimes is meant to refer to the steady commercial growth of the Internet with the advent of the world wide web as exemplified by the first release of the Mosaic web browser in 1993 and continuing through the 1990s.

The period was marked by the founding (and, in many cases, spectacular failure) of a group of new Internet-based companies commonly referred to as dot-coms.

Zoning

Zoning is a device of land use regulation used by local governments in most developed countries. Zoning may be use-based, or it may regulate building height, lot coverage, and similar characteristics, or some combination of these.

Theoretically, the primary purpose of Zoning is to segregate uses that are thought to be incompatible.

Crisis

A Crisis may occur on a personal or societal level. It may be an unstable and dangerous social situation, in political, social, economic, military affairs, or a large-scale environmental event, especially one involving an impending abrupt change. More loosely, it is a term meaning "a testing time" or "emergency event".

Solution

In chemistry, a Solution is a homogeneous mixture composed of two or more substances. In such a mixture, a solute is dissolved in another substance, known as a solvent. Gases may dissolve in liquids, for example, carbon dioxide or oxygen in water.

Chapter 9. TOPICS IN THE ECONOMICS OF TORT LIABILITY

Chapter 10. AN ECONOMIC THEORY OF THE LEGAL PROCESS

Social	The term social refers to a characteristic of living organisms (humans in particular, though biologists also apply the term to populations of other animals). It always refers to the interaction of organisms with other organisms and to their collective co-existence, irrespective of whether they are aware of it or not, and irrespective of whether the interaction is voluntary or involuntary. In the absence of agreement about its meaning, the term "ps" is used in many different senses and regarded as a [[]], referringse among other things to: · Attitudes, orientations, or behaviours which take the interests, intentions, or needs of other people into account (in contrast to anti-social behaviour);has played some role in defining the idea or the principle. For instance terms like social realism, social justice, social constructivism, social psychology and social capital imply that there is some social process involved or considered, a process that is not there in regular, "non-social", realism, justice, constructivism, psychology, or capital.
Social cost	In neoclassical economics social cost is defined as the sum of private and external costs. Neoclassical economic theorists ascribe individual decision-making to a calculation costs and benefits. Rational choice theory assumes that individuals only consider their own private costs when making decisions, not the costs that may be borne by others.
Calendar	A Calendar is a system of organizing days for social, religious, commercial, typically days, weeks, months, and years. The name given to each day is known as a date.
Decision tree	A decision tree (or tree diagram) is a decision support tool that uses a tree-like graph or model of decisions and their possible consequences, including chance event outcomes, resource costs, and utility. decision trees are commonly used in operations research, specifically in decision analysis, to help identify a strategy most likely to reach a goal. Another use of decision trees is as a descriptive means for calculating conditional probabilities.
Expected value	In probability theory and statistics, the Expected value (or expectation value, or mean, or first moment) of a random variable is the integral of the random variable with respect to its probability measure. For discrete random variables this is equivalent to the probability-weighted sum of the possible values. For continuous random variables with a density function it is the probability density-weighted integral of the possible values.
Dot-com bubble	The "Dot-com bubble" (or) was a speculative bubble covering roughly 1998-2001 (with a climax on March 10, 2000 with the NASDAQ peaking at 5132.52) during which stock markets in Western nations saw their equity value rise rapidly from growth in the more recent Internet sector and related fields. While the latter part was a boom and bust cycle, the Internet boom sometimes is meant to refer to the steady commercial growth of the Internet with the advent of the world wide web as exemplified by the first release of the Mosaic web browser in 1993 and continuing through the 1990s. The period was marked by the founding (and, in many cases, spectacular failure) of a group of new Internet-based companies commonly referred to as dot-coms.
Appeal	In law, an appeal is a process for requesting a formal change to an official decision.

Chapter 10. AN ECONOMIC THEORY OF THE LEGAL PROCESS

Chapter 10. AN ECONOMIC THEORY OF THE LEGAL PROCESS

	The specific procedures for appealing, including even whether there is a right of appeal from a particular type of decision, can vary greatly from country to country. Even within a jurisdiction, the nature of an appeal can vary greatly depending on the type of case.
Authorization hold	Authorization hold (also card authorisation, preauthorization) is the practice within the banking industry of authorizing electronic transactions done with a debit card or credit card and holding this balance as unavailable either until the merchant clears the transaction, or the hold "falls off." In the case of debit cards, Authorization holds can fall off the account (thus rendering the balance available again) anywhere from 1-5 days after the transaction date depending on the bank"s policy; in the case of credit cards, holds may last as long as 30 days, depending on the issuing bank. Signature-based (non-PIN-based) credit and debit card transactions are a two-step process, consisting of an authorization and a settlement. When a merchant swipes a customer"s credit card, the credit card terminal connects to the merchant"s acquirer, or credit card processor, which verifies that the customer"s account is valid and that sufficient funds are available to cover the transaction"s cost.
Bargaining	Bargaining or haggling is a type of negotiation in which the buyer and seller of a good or service dispute the price which will be paid and the exact nature of the transaction that will take place, and eventually come to an agreement. Bargaining is an alternative pricing strategy to fixed prices. Optimally, if it costs the retailer nothing to engage and allow Bargaining, he can divine the buyer"s willingness to spend.
Damages	In law, Damages are money claimed by or ordered to be paid to a person as compensation for loss or injury. Compensatory Damages, also called actual Damages, are paid to compensate the claimant for loss, injury, or harm suffered by another"s breach of duty. On a breach of contract by a defendant, a court generally awards the sum that would restore the injured party to the economic position they expected from performance of the promise or promises (known as an "expectation measure" or "benefit-of-the-bargain" measure of Damages).
Causality	Causality refers to the relationship between an event (the cause) and a second event (the effect), where the second event is a direct consequence of the first. The philosophical treatment of Causality extends over millennia. In the Western philosophical tradition, discussion stretches back at least to Aristotle, and the topic remains a staple in contemporary philosophy.
Trial	In law, a trial is when parties come together to a dispute present information (in the form of evidence) in a formal setting, usually a court, before a judge, jury, in order to achieve a resolution to their dispute.

Chapter 10. AN ECONOMIC THEORY OF THE LEGAL PROCESS

· Where the trial is held before a group of members of the community, it is called a jury trial.
· Where the trial is held solely before a judge, it is called a bench trial. Bench trials involve fewer formalities, and are typically resolved faster. Furthermore, a favorable ruling for one party in a bench trial will frequently lead the other party to offer a settlement.

Contract

In common-law systems, the five key requirements for the creation of a contract are: 1. offer and acceptance (agreement) 2. consideration 3. an intention to create legal relations 4. legal capacity 5. formalities

In civil-law systems, the concept of consideration is not central. In addition, for some contracts formalities must be complied with under what is sometimes called a statute of frauds.

One of the most famous cases on forming a contract is Carlill v. Carbolic Smoke Ball Company, decided in nineteenth-century England.

Fiefdom

Under the system of medieval European feudalism, a Fiefdom, fief, feud, feoff, often consisted of inheritable lands or revenue-producing property granted by a liege lord, generally to a vassal, in return for a form of allegiance, originally to give him the means to fulfill his military duties when called upon. However, anything of value could be held in fief, such as an office, a right of exploitation (e.g., hunting, fishing) or any other type of revenue, rather than the land it comes from.

Originally, the feudal institution of vassalage did not imply the giving or receiving of landholdings (which were granted only as a reward for loyalty), but by the eighth century the giving of a landholding was becoming standard.

Chief brand officer

A Chief brand officer is a relatively new executive level position at a corporation, company, organization, typically reporting directly to the CEO or board of directors. The Chief brand officer is responsible for a brand"s image, experience, and promise, and propagating it throughout all aspects of the company. The brand officer oversees marketing, advertising, design, public relations and customer service departments. The brand equity of a company is seen as becoming increasingly dependent on the role of a Chief brand officer.

Companies that currently employ a Chief brand officer include:

· Srinivas Kumar, Baskin-Robbins Worldwide
· Michael Keller, Dairy Queen
· Will Kussell, Dunkin" Brands, Inc.
· Trey Hall, Boston Market Corporation
· Allen Schiffenbaure, G 2 Marketing Group
· Alan Bergstrom, Storyminers Inc.
· Brian Igoe, Metabolix, Inc.
· Phil Mcaveety, Luxury Collection
· Mark I. McCallum, Brown-Forman Corporation
· Phil McAveety, Starwood Hotels ' Resorts Worldwide, Inc.
· Danny Meisenheimer, Souper Salad, Inc

Chapter 10. AN ECONOMIC THEORY OF THE LEGAL PROCESS

Markets	A market is any one of a variety of different systems, institutions, procedures, social relations and infrastructures whereby persons trade, and goods and services are exchanged, forming part of the economy. It is an arrangement that allows buyers and sellers to exchange things. markets vary in size, range, geographic scale, location, types and variety of human communities, as well as the types of goods and services traded.
Incentive	In economics and sociology, an Incentive is any factor (financial or non-financial) that enables or motivates a particular course of action, the study of Incentive structures is central to the study of all economic activity (both in terms of individual decision-making and in terms of co-operation and competition within a larger institutional structure).
Elasticity	In economics, elasticity is the ratio of the percent change in one variable to the percent change in another variable. It is a tool for measuring the responsiveness of a function to changes in parameters in a relative way. Commonly analyzed are elasticity of substitution, price and wealth.
Inelastic demand	Perfectly inelastic demand Perfectly elastic demand A price fall usually results in an increase in the quantity demanded by consumers . The demand for a good is relatively inelastic when the change in quantity demanded is less than change in price. Goods and services for which no substitutes exist are generally inelastic.
Information	Information as a concept has many meanings, from everyday usage to technical settings. The concept of Information is closely related to notions of constraint, communication, control, data, form, instruction, knowledge, meaning, mental stimulus, pattern, perception, and representation. The English word was apparently derived from the Latin accusative form of the nominative (informatio): this noun is in its turn derived from the verb "informare" (to inform) in the sense of "to give form to the mind", "to discipline", "instruct", "teach": "Men so wise should go and inform their kings." (1330) Inform itself comes from the Latin verb informare, to give form to, to form an idea of.
Elawyering	The term Elawyering or e-lawyering is a neologism used to refer to the practice of law over the Internet, in a way more expansive than a mere legal related internet advertisement for a service, lawyer, Elawyering initiatives have been undertaken by the American Bar Association in order to reach a "latent market" of lower and middle class citizens in need of legal services. Lawyers practicing law online are also referred to as "virtual lawyers" and practice from virtual law offices.
Stock split	A Stock split or stock divide increases or decreases the number of shares in a public company. The price is adjusted such that the market capitalization of the company remains the same after the split, so that dilution does not occur. Options and warrants are included.
Job interview	A Job interview is a process in which a potential employee is evaluated by an employer for prospective employment in their company, organization, and was established in the late 16th century. A Job interview typically precedes the hiring decision, and is used to evaluate the candidate. The interview is usually preceded by the evaluation of submitted résumés from interested candidates, then selecting a small number of candidates for interviews.

Chapter 10. AN ECONOMIC THEORY OF THE LEGAL PROCESS

Chapter 10. AN ECONOMIC THEORY OF THE LEGAL PROCESS

Optimism	Optimism is "an inclination to put the most favorable construction upon actions and events or to anticipate the best possible outcome". It is the philosophical opposite of pessimism. Optimists generally believe that people and events are inherently good, so that most situations work out in the end for the best.
Loss aversion	In prospect theory, Loss aversion refers to people"s tendency to strongly prefer avoiding losses to acquiring gains. Some studies suggest that losses are twice as powerful, psychologically, as gains. Loss aversion was first convincingly demonstrated by Amos Tversky and Daniel Kahneman.
Rights	Rights are entitlements or permissions, usually of a legal or moral nature. rights are of vital importance in the fields of law and ethics, especially theories of justice and deontology. There are numerous different theoretical distinctions in accordance with which rights may be classified.
Cooperative	A cooperative (also co-operative or coöperative; often referred to as a co-op or coop) is defined by the International Co-operative Alliance"s Statement on the Co-operative Identity as an autonomous association of persons united voluntarily to meet their common economic, social, and cultural needs and aspirations through a jointly-owned and democratically-controlled enterprise. It is a business organization owned and operated by a group of individuals for their mutual benefit. A cooperative may also be defined as a business owned and controlled equally by the people who use its services or who work at it.
Suit	A suit is a set of garments crafted from the same cloth, consisting of at least a jacket and trousers. Lounge suits are the most common style of Western suit, originating in England as country wear. Other types of suit still worn today are firstly the dinner suit, part of black tie, which arose as a lounging alternative to dress coats in much the same way as the day lounge suit came to replace frock and morning coats; and secondly, rarely worn today, the morning suit.
Alternative dispute resolution	Alternative dispute resolution (also known as External Dispute Resolution in some countries, such as Australia) includes dispute resolution processes and techniques that fall outside of the government judicial process. Despite historic resistance to Alternative dispute resolution by both parties and their advocates, Alternative dispute resolution has gained widespread acceptance among both the general public and the legal profession in recent years. In fact, some courts now require some parties to resort to Alternative dispute resolution of some type, usually mediation, before permitting the parties" cases to be tried.
Arbitration	Arbitration, a form of alternative dispute resolution (ADR), is a legal technique for the resolution of disputes outside the courts, wherein the parties to a dispute refer it to one or more persons (the "arbitrators", "arbiters" or "arbitral tribunal"), by whose decision (the "award") they agree to be bound. It is a settlement technique in which a third party reviews the case and imposes a decision that is legally binding for both sides. Other forms of ADR include mediation (a form of settlement negotiation facilitated by a neutral third party) and non-binding resolution by experts.

Chapter 10. AN ECONOMIC THEORY OF THE LEGAL PROCESS

Chapter 10. AN ECONOMIC THEORY OF THE LEGAL PROCESS

Compulsory arbitration	Compulsory arbitration. In labor disputes, some laws of some communities force the two sides labor and management, to undergo arbitration. These laws mostly apply when the possibility of a strike seriously affects the public interest.
Invisible hand	In economics, the Invisible hand, also known as the Invisible hand of the market, the term economists use to describe the self-regulating nature of the marketplace, is a metaphor first coined by the economist Adam Smith in The Theory of Moral Sentiments. For Smith, the Invisible hand was created by the conjunction of the forces of self-interest, competition, and supply and demand, which he noted as being capable of allocating resources in society. This is the founding justification for the laissez-faire economic philosophy.
Compromise	Cultural background and influences, the meaning and perception of the word "Compromise" may be different: In the UK, Ireland and Commonwealth countries the word "Compromise" has a positive meaning (as a consent, an agreement where both parties win something); in the USA it may rather have negative connotations (as both parties lose something). Defining and finding the best possible Compromise is an important problem in fields like game theory and the voting system. Research has indicated that suboptimal Compromises are often the result of negotiators failing to realize when they have interests that are completely compatible with those of the other party and settle for suboptimal agreements.
Economies of scope	Economies of scope are conceptually similar to economies of scale. Whereas economies of scale primarily refer to efficiencies associated with supply-side changes, such as increasing or decreasing the scale of production, of a single product type, Economies of scope refer to efficiencies primarily associated with demand-side changes, such as increasing or decreasing the scope of marketing and distribution, of different types of products. Economies of scope are one of the main reasons for such marketing strategies as product bundling, product lining, and family branding.
Liability	In financial accounting, a Liability is defined as an obligation of an entity arising from past transactions or events, the settlement of which may result in the transfer or use of assets, provision of services or other yielding of economic benefits in the future. · All type of borrowing from persons or banks for improving a business or person income which is payable during short or long time. · They embody a duty or responsibility to others that entails settlement by future transfer or use of assets, provision of services or other yielding of economic benefits, at a specified or determinable date, on occurrence of a specified event, or on demand; · The duty or responsibility obligates the entity leaving it little or no discretion to avoid it; and, · The transaction or event obligating the entity has already occurred. Liabilities in financial accounting need not be legally enforceable; but can be based on equitable obligations or constructive obligations. An equitable obligation is a duty based on ethical or moral considerations.

Chapter 10. AN ECONOMIC THEORY OF THE LEGAL PROCESS

Chapter 10. AN ECONOMIC THEORY OF THE LEGAL PROCESS

Burden of proof	The Burden of proof is the obligation to shift the assumed conclusion away from an oppositional opinion to one"s own position. The Burden of proof may only be fulfilled by evidence. The Burden of proof is often associated with the Latin maxim semper necessitas probandi incumbit ei qui agit, the best translation of which seems to be: "the necessity of proof always lies with the person who lays charges." This is a statement of a version of the presumption of innocence which underpins the assessment of evidence in some legal systems, and is not a general statement of when one takes on the Burden of proof.
Decision theory	Decision theory in mathematics and statistics is concerned with identifying the values, uncertainties and other issues relevant in a given decision and the resulting optimal decision. It is very closely related to the field of game theory. Most of decision theory is normative or prescriptive, i.e., it is concerned with identifying the best decision to take, assuming an ideal decision maker who is fully informed, able to compute with perfect accuracy, and fully rational.
Supreme Court	A Supreme Court (, court of final appeal or high court) is in some jurisdictions the highest judicial body within that jurisdiction"s court system, whose rulings are not subject to further review by another court. The designations for such courts differ among jurisdictions. Courts of last resort typically function primarily as appellate courts, hearing appeals from the lower trial courts or intermediate-level appellate courts.
Coase Theorem	In law and economics, the Coase theorem, attributed to Ronald Coase, describes the economic efficiency of an economic allocation or outcome in the presence of externalities. The theorem states that when trade in an externality is possible and there are no transaction costs, bargaining will lead to an efficient outcome regardless of the initial allocation of property rights. In practice, obstacles to bargaining or poorly defined property rights can prevent Coasian bargaining.
Regulation	Regulation refers to "controlling human or societal behaviour by rules or restrictions." Regulation can take many forms: legal restrictions promulgated by a government authority, self-Regulation, social Regulation (e.g. norms), co-Regulation and market Regulation. One can consider Regulation as actions of conduct imposing sanctions (such as a fine). This action of administrative law, or implementing regulatory law, may be contrasted with statutory or case law.
Functional selectivity	Functional selectivity (or "agonist trafficking", "biased agonism", "differential engagement" and "protean agonism") is the ligand-dependent selectivity for certain signal transduction pathways in one and the same receptor. This can be present when a receptor has several possible signal transduction pathways. To which degree each pathway is activated thus depends on which ligand binds to the receptor .
Tort	Tort law is a body of law that addresses, and provides remedies for, civil wrongs not arising out of contractual obligations. A person who suffers legal damages may be able to use Tort law to receive compensation from someone who is legally responsible, or liable, for those injuries. Generally speaking, Tort law defines what constitutes a legal injury and establishes the circumstances under which one person may be held liable for another"s injury.

Chapter 10. AN ECONOMIC THEORY OF THE LEGAL PROCESS

Chapter 10. AN ECONOMIC THEORY OF THE LEGAL PROCESS

Anecdotal value	In economics, Anecdotal value refers to the primarily social and political value of an anecdote or anecdotal evidence in promoting understanding of a social, cultural, in the last several decades the evaluation of anecdotes has received sustained academic scrutiny from economists and scholars such as S.G. Checkland (on David Ricardo), Steven Novella, Hollis Robbins, R. Charleton, Kwamena Kwansah-Aidoo, and others; these academics seek to quantify the value inherent in the deployment of anecdotes. More recently, economists studying choice models have begun assessing Anecdotal value in the context of framing; Kahneman and Tversky suggest that choice models may be contingent on stories or anecdotes that frame or influence choice.
Hierarchy	A hierarchy is an arrangement of items (objects, names, values, categories, etc). in which the items are represented as being "above," "below," or "at the same level as" one another and with only one "neighbour" above and below each level. These classifications are made with regard to rank, importance, seniority, power status or authority.
Code	In communications, a Code is a rule for converting a piece of information (for example, a letter, word, phrase) into another form or representation (one sign into another sign), not necessarily of the same type. In communications and information processing, encoding is the process by which information from a source is converted into symbols to be communicated. Decoding is the reverse process, converting these Code symbols back into information understandable by a receiver.
Mercantile	Mercantile (or Commercial) Agencies, is the name given in United States to organizations designed to collect, record and distribute to regular clients information relative to the standing of commercial firms. In Great Britain and some European countries trade protective societies, composed of merchants and tradesmen, are formed for the promotion of trade, and members exchange information regarding the standing of business houses. These societies had their origin in the associations formed in the middle of the 18th century for the purpose of disseminating information regarding bankruptcies, assignments and bills of sale.
Uniform Commercial Code	The Uniform Commercial Code (Uniform Commercial Code or the Code), first published in 1952, is one of a number of uniform acts that have been promulgated in conjunction with efforts to harmonize the law of sales and other commercial transactions in all 50 states within the United States of America. This objective is deemed important because of the prevalence of commercial transactions that extend beyond one state . If the Uniform Commercial Code had not been adopted, it is likely that the Congress of the United States, exercising its authority under the Commerce Clause of the United States Constitution would have enacted national legislation. The Uniform Commercial Code therefore achieved the goal of achieving substantial uniformity in commercial legislation and, at the same time, allowed the states needed flexibility to meet local circumstances.
Voluntary association	A Voluntary association or union (also , unincorporated association) is a group of individuals who voluntarily enter into an agreement to form a body (or organization) to accomplish a purpose. Strictly speaking in many jurisdictions no formalities are necessary to start an association. In some jurisdictions, there is a minimum for the number of persons starting an association.

Chapter 10. AN ECONOMIC THEORY OF THE LEGAL PROCESS

Chapter 10. AN ECONOMIC THEORY OF THE LEGAL PROCESS

Comparative negligence	Comparative negligence, is a partial legal defense that reduces the amount of damages that a plaintiff can recover in a negligence-based claim based upon the degree to which the plaintiff's own negligence contributed to cause the injury. When the defense is asserted, the fact-finder, usually a jury, must decide the degree to which the plaintiff's negligence versus the combined negligence of all other relevant actors contributed to cause the plaintiff's damages. It is a modification of the doctrine of contributory negligence which disallows any recovery by a plaintiff whose negligence contributed, even minimally, to causing the damages.
Pareto efficiency	Pareto efficiency, is an important concept in economics with broad applications in game theory, engineering and the social sciences. The term is named after Vilfredo Pareto, an Italian economist who used the concept in his studies of economic efficiency and income distribution. Informally, Pareto efficient situations are those in which any change to make any person better off is impossible without making someone else worse off.
Long-run	In economic models, the long-run time frame assumes no fixed factors of production. Firms can enter or leave the marketplace, and the cost (and availability) of land, labor, raw materials, and capital goods can be assumed to vary. In contrast, in the short-run time frame, certain factors are assumed to be fixed, because there is not sufficient time for them to change.
Selection effect	Selection bias (e.g. Berkson"s bias) is a statistical bias is which there is an error in choosing the individuals or groups to take part in a scientific study. It is sometimes referred to as the Selection effect. The term "selection bias" most often refers to the distortion of a statistical analysis, resulting from the method of collecting samples.
Nominative determinism	Nominative determinism refers to the theory that a person"s name is given an influential role in reflecting key attributes of his job, profession, but real examples are more highly prized, the more obscure the better.
Shopping	Shopping is the examining of goods or services from retailers with the intent to purchase at that time. Shopping is an activity of selection and/or purchase. In some contexts it is considered a leisure activity as well as an economic one.
Mediation	Mediation, a form of alternative dispute resolution (ADR) or "appropriate dispute resolution", aims to assist two (or more) disputants in reaching an agreement. The parties themselves determine the conditions of any settlements reached-- rather than accepting something imposed by a third party. The disputes may involve (as parties) states, organizations, communities, individuals or other representatives with a vested interest in the outcome.

Chapter 10. AN ECONOMIC THEORY OF THE LEGAL PROCESS

Chapter 11. AN ECONOMIC THEORY OF CRIME AND PUNISHMENT

Anecdotal value	In economics, Anecdotal value refers to the primarily social and political value of an anecdote or anecdotal evidence in promoting understanding of a social, cultural, in the last several decades the evaluation of anecdotes has received sustained academic scrutiny from economists and scholars such as S.G. Checkland (on David Ricardo), Steven Novella, Hollis Robbins, R. Charleton, Kwamena Kwansah-Aidoo, and others; these academics seek to quantify the value inherent in the deployment of anecdotes. More recently, economists studying choice models have begun assessing Anecdotal value in the context of framing; Kahneman and Tversky suggest that choice models may be contingent on stories or anecdotes that frame or influence choice.
Elawyering	The term Elawyering or e-lawyering is a neologism used to refer to the practice of law over the Internet, in a way more expansive than a mere legal related internet advertisement for a service, lawyer, Elawyering initiatives have been undertaken by the American Bar Association in order to reach a "latent market" of lower and middle class citizens in need of legal services. Lawyers practicing law online are also referred to as "virtual lawyers" and practice from virtual law offices.
Statute	A statute is a formal written enactment of a legislative authority that governs a country, state, city, or county. Typically, statutes command or prohibit something, or declare policy. The word is often used to distinguish law made by legislative bodies from case law and the regulations issued by Government agencies.
Reasonable doubt	If doubt does affect a "reasonable person"s" belief that the defendant is guilty, the jury is not satisfied beyond a "Reasonable doubt". The precise meaning of words such as "reasonable" and "doubt" are usually defined within jurisprudence of the applicable country. The use of "Reasonable doubt" as a standard requirement in the western justice system originated in medieval England.
Limitations	A statute of limitations is a statute in a common law legal system that sets forth the maximum period of time, after certain events, that legal proceedings based on those events may be initiated. In civil law systems, similar provisions are usually part of the civil code or criminal code and are often known collectively as "periods of prescription" or "prescriptive periods." Common law legal system might have a statute limiting the time for prosecution of crimes called misdemeanors to two years after the offense occurred. In that statute, if a person is discovered to have committed a misdemeanor three years ago, the time has expired for the prosecution of the misdemeanor.
Cost	In business, retail, and accounting, a cost is the value of money that has been used up to produce something, and hence is not available for use anymore. In economics, a cost is an alternative that is given up as a result of a decision. In business, the cost may be one of acquisition, in which case the amount of money expended to acquire it is counted as cost.

Chapter 11. AN ECONOMIC THEORY OF CRIME AND PUNISHMENT

Chapter 11. AN ECONOMIC THEORY OF CRIME AND PUNISHMENT

External	In economics, an externality or spillover of an economic transaction is an impact on a party that is not directly involved in the transaction. In such a case, prices do not reflect the full costs or benefits in production or consumption of a product or service. An advantageous impact is called an external benefit or positive externality, while a detrimental impact is called an external cost or negative externality.
Theory of the firm	The Theory of the firm consists of a number of economic theories which describe the nature of the firm, company, including its existence, its behaviour, and its relationship with the market. In simplified terms, the Theory of the firm aims to answer these questions: · Existence - why do firms emerge, why are not all transactions in the economy mediated over the market? · Boundaries - why the boundary between firms and the market is located exactly there? Which transactions are performed internally and which are negotiated on the market? · Organization - why are firms structured in such a specific way? What is the interplay of formal and informal relationships? The First World War period saw a change of emphasis in economic theory away from industry-level analysis which mainly included analysing markets to analysis at the level of the firm, as it became increasingly clear that perfect competition was no longer an adequate model of how firms behaved. Economic theory till then had focused on trying to understand markets alone and there had been little study on understanding why firms or organisations exist. Markets are mainly guided by prices as illustrated by vegetable markets where a buyer is free to switch sellers in an exchange.
Demand	In economics, demand is the desire to own anything and the ability to pay for it. . The term demand signifies the ability or the willingness to buy a particular commodity at a given point of time.
Future	Futures may mean: · Futures contract, a tradable financial contract · Futures exchange, a financial market where Futures contracts are traded · Futures (magazine), an American finance magazine · Futures studies, multidisciplinary studies of patterns to determine the likelihood of Future trends · Futures (journal), an international Futures studies journal · Futures (album), a 2004 release by Jimmy Eat World · "Futures" (song), a single from the above album · Futures and promises, computer programming objects that act as proxies for results that are not yet determined · Futures tournaments, minor professional tennis events .

Chapter 11. AN ECONOMIC THEORY OF CRIME AND PUNISHMENT

Chapter 11. AN ECONOMIC THEORY OF CRIME AND PUNISHMENT

Social	The term social refers to a characteristic of living organisms (humans in particular, though biologists also apply the term to populations of other animals). It always refers to the interaction of organisms with other organisms and to their collective co-existence, irrespective of whether they are aware of it or not, and irrespective of whether the interaction is voluntary or involuntary. In the absence of agreement about its meaning, the term "ps" is used in many different senses and regarded as a [[]], referringse among other things to: · Attitudes, orientations, or behaviours which take the interests, intentions, or needs of other people into account (in contrast to anti-social behaviour);has played some role in defining the idea or the principle. For instance terms like social realism, social justice, social constructivism, social psychology and social capital imply that there is some social process involved or considered, a process that is not there in regular, "non-social", realism, justice, constructivism, psychology, or capital.
Social cost	In neoclassical economics social cost is defined as the sum of private and external costs. Neoclassical economic theorists ascribe individual decision-making to a calculation costs and benefits. Rational choice theory assumes that individuals only consider their own private costs when making decisions, not the costs that may be borne by others.
Michael Robert Milken	Michael Robert Milken is an American financier and philanthropist noted for his role in the development of the market for high-yield bonds during the 1970s and 1980s, for his 1990 guilty plea to multiple felony charges that he violated US securities laws, and for his funding of medical research. Milken was indicted on 98 counts of racketeering and securities fraud in 1989 as the result of an insider trading investigation. After a plea bargain, he pled guilty to six securities and reporting violations but was never convicted of racketeering or insider trading.
Bond	In finance, a Bond is a debt security, in which the authorized issuer owes the holders a debt and, depending on the terms of the Bond, is obliged to pay interest (the coupon) and/or to repay the principal at a later date, termed maturity. A Bond is a formal contract to repay borrowed money with interest at fixed intervals. Thus a Bond is like a loan: the issuer is the borrower (debtor), the holder is the lender (creditor), and the coupon is the interest.
Controllability	Controllability is an important property of a control system, and the Controllability property plays a crucial role in many control problems, such as stabilization of unstable systems by feedback, the concept of Controllability denotes the ability to move a system around in its entire configuration space using only certain admissible manipulations.
Mean	In statistics, mean has two related meanings: · the arithmetic mean . · the expected value of a random variable, which is also called the population mean.

Chapter 11. AN ECONOMIC THEORY OF CRIME AND PUNISHMENT

Chapter 11. AN ECONOMIC THEORY OF CRIME AND PUNISHMENT

	It is sometimes stated that the "mean" means average. This is incorrect if "mean" is taken in the specific sense of "arithmetic mean" as there are different types of averages: the mean, median, and mode.
Insurance	Insurance, in law and economics, is a form of risk management primarily used to hedge against the risk of a contingent loss. Insurance is defined as the equitable transfer of the risk of a loss, from one entity to another, in exchange for a premium, and can be thought of as a guaranteed and known small loss to prevent a large, possibly devastating loss. An insurer is a company selling the Insurance; an insured or policyholder is the person or entity buying the Insurance.
Ex-ante	The term ex-ante is a neo-Latin word meaning "before the event". ex-ante is used most commonly in the commercial world, where results of a particular action, or series of actions, are forecast in advance. The opposite of ex-ante is ex-post (or ex post).
Observable	In physics, particularly in quantum physics, a system observable is a property of the system state that can be determined by some sequence of physical operations. For example, these operations might involve submitting the system to various electromagnetic fields and eventually reading a value off some gauge. In systems governed by classical mechanics, any experimentally observable value can be shown to be given by a real-valued function on the set of all possible system states.

Chapter 11. AN ECONOMIC THEORY OF CRIME AND PUNISHMENT

Chapter 12. TOPICS IN THE ECONOMICS OF CRIME AND PUNISHMENT

United States	The United States of America (commonly referred to as the United States, the U.S., the USA) is a federal constitutional republic comprising fifty states and a federal district. The country is situated mostly in central North America, where its forty-eight contiguous states and Washington, D.C., the capital district, lie between the Pacific and Atlantic Oceans, bordered by Canada to the north and Mexico to the south. The state of Alaska is in the northwest of the continent, with Canada to the east and Russia to the west across the Bering Strait.
Anecdotal value	In economics, Anecdotal value refers to the primarily social and political value of an anecdote or anecdotal evidence in promoting understanding of a social, cultural, in the last several decades the evaluation of anecdotes has received sustained academic scrutiny from economists and scholars such as S.G. Checkland (on David Ricardo), Steven Novella, Hollis Robbins, R. Charleton, Kwamena Kwansah-Aidoo, and others; these academics seek to quantify the value inherent in the deployment of anecdotes. More recently, economists studying choice models have begun assessing Anecdotal value in the context of framing; Kahneman and Tversky suggest that choice models may be contingent on stories or anecdotes that frame or influence choice.
Liability	In financial accounting, a Liability is defined as an obligation of an entity arising from past transactions or events, the settlement of which may result in the transfer or use of assets, provision of services or other yielding of economic benefits in the future. · All type of borrowing from persons or banks for improving a business or person income which is payable during short or long time. · They embody a duty or responsibility to others that entails settlement by future transfer or use of assets, provision of services or other yielding of economic benefits, at a specified or determinable date, on occurrence of a specified event, or on demand; · The duty or responsibility obligates the entity leaving it little or no discretion to avoid it; and, · The transaction or event obligating the entity has already occurred. Liabilities in financial accounting need not be legally enforceable; but can be based on equitable obligations or constructive obligations. An equitable obligation is a duty based on ethical or moral considerations.
Statistics	Statistics is a branch of mathematics concerned with collecting and interpreting data. According to other definitions, it is a mathematical science pertaining to the collection, analysis, interpretation or explanation, and presentation of data. Statisticians improve the quality of data with the design of experiments and survey sampling.
Dot-com bubble	The "Dot-com bubble" (or) was a speculative bubble covering roughly 1998-2001 (with a climax on March 10, 2000 with the NASDAQ peaking at 5132.52) during which stock markets in Western nations saw their equity value rise rapidly from growth in the more recent Internet sector and related fields. While the latter part was a boom and bust cycle, the Internet boom sometimes is meant to refer to the steady commercial growth of the Internet with the advent of the world wide web as exemplified by the first release of the Mosaic web browser in 1993 and continuing through the 1990s. The period was marked by the founding (and, in many cases, spectacular failure) of a group of new Internet-based companies commonly referred to as dot-coms.

Chapter 12. TOPICS IN THE ECONOMICS OF CRIME AND PUNISHMENT

Chapter 12. TOPICS IN THE ECONOMICS OF CRIME AND PUNISHMENT

Trend analysis	The term "trend analysis" refers to the concept of collecting information and attempting to spot a pattern, in the information. In some fields of study, the term "trend analysis" has more formally-defined meanings. In project management trend analysis is a mathematical technique that uses historical results to predict future outcome.
Poverty	Poverty is the condition of lacking basic human needs such as nutrition, clean water, health care, clothing, and shelter because of the inability to afford them. This is also referred to as absolute Poverty or destitution. Relative Poverty is the condition of having resources or less income than others within a society or country, or compared to worldwide averages.
Cost	In business, retail, and accounting, a cost is the value of money that has been used up to produce something, and hence is not available for use anymore. In economics, a cost is an alternative that is given up as a result of a decision. In business, the cost may be one of acquisition, in which case the amount of money expended to acquire it is counted as cost.
Social	The term social refers to a characteristic of living organisms (humans in particular, though biologists also apply the term to populations of other animals). It always refers to the interaction of organisms with other organisms and to their collective co-existence, irrespective of whether they are aware of it or not, and irrespective of whether the interaction is voluntary or involuntary. In the absence of agreement about its meaning, the term "ps" is used in many different senses and regarded as a [[]], referringse among other things to: · Attitudes, orientations, or behaviours which take the interests, intentions, or needs of other people into account (in contrast to anti-social behaviour);has played some role in defining the idea or the principle. For instance terms like social realism, social justice, social constructivism, social psychology and social capital imply that there is some social process involved or considered, a process that is not there in regular, "non-social", realism, justice, constructivism, psychology, or capital.
Social cost	In neoclassical economics social cost is defined as the sum of private and external costs. Neoclassical economic theorists ascribe individual decision-making to a calculation costs and benefits. Rational choice theory assumes that individuals only consider their own private costs when making decisions, not the costs that may be borne by others.
Hypothesis	A hypothesis is a proposed explanation for an observable phenomenon. The term derives from the Greek, hypotithenai meaning "to put under" or "to suppose." For a hypothesis to be put forward as a scientific hypothesis, the scientific method requires that one can test it. Scientists generally base scientific hypotheses on previous observations that cannot be satisfactorily explained with the available scientific theories.

Chapter 12. TOPICS IN THE ECONOMICS OF CRIME AND PUNISHMENT

Chapter 12. TOPICS IN THE ECONOMICS OF CRIME AND PUNISHMENT

Functional selectivity	Functional selectivity (or "agonist trafficking", "biased agonism", "differential engagement" and "protean agonism") is the ligand-dependent selectivity for certain signal transduction pathways in one and the same receptor. This can be present when a receptor has several possible signal transduction pathways. To which degree each pathway is activated thus depends on which ligand binds to the receptor.
Saleability	Saleability is a technical analysis term used to compare performances of different trading systems or different investments within one system. Note, it is not simply another word for profit. There are varying definitions for it, some as simple as the expected or average ratio of revenue to cost for a particular investment or trading system or "ratio of the number of winning trades or investments to the total number of trades or investments made, a number ranging from zero to 1." Others can be complex or counter-intuitive.
Elawyering	The term Elawyering or e-lawyering is a neologism used to refer to the practice of law over the Internet, in a way more expansive than a mere legal related internet advertisement for a service, lawyer, Elawyering initiatives have been undertaken by the American Bar Association in order to reach a "latent market" of lower and middle class citizens in need of legal services. Lawyers practicing law online are also referred to as "virtual lawyers" and practice from virtual law offices.
Fence	A Fence is a freestanding structure designed to restrict or prevent movement across a boundary. It is generally distinguished from a wall by the lightness of its construction: a wall is usually restricted to such barriers made from solid brick or concrete, blocking vision as well as passage (though the definitions overlap somewhat). Fences are constructed for several purposes, including: · Agricultural fencing, to keep livestock in or predators out · Privacy fencing, to provide privacy · Temporary fencing, to provide safety and security, and to direct movement, wherever temporary access control is required, especially on building and construction sites · Perimeter fencing, to prevent trespassing or theft and/or to keep children and pets from wandering away. · Decorative fencing, to enhance the appearance of a property, garden or other landscaping · Boundary fencing, to demarcate a piece of real property Typical agricultural barbed wire fencing. Split-rail fencing common in timber-rich areas. Chain link Fence surrounding a field in Jurong, Singapore. Various types of fencing include:

Chapter 12. TOPICS IN THE ECONOMICS OF CRIME AND PUNISHMENT

Chapter 12. TOPICS IN THE ECONOMICS OF CRIME AND PUNISHMENT

- Aluminum
- Barbed wire Fence
- Cactus Fence
- Chain link fencing, sometimes called "wire netting"
- Concrete Fence, easy to install and highly durable
- Chicken wire, light wire mesh for keeping predators out and chickens or other small livestock in
- Dry-stone wall or rock Fence, often agricultural
- Electric Fence
- Ha-ha (or sunken Fence)
- Hedgerows of intertwined, living shrubs (constructed by hedge laying)
- High tensile smooth wire
- Hurdle fencing, made from moveable sections
- Live fencing is the use of live woody species for Fences.
- Palisade
- Pest-exclusion Fence
- Pet Fence Underground Fence for pet containment
- Picket Fences, generally a waist-high, painted, partially decorative Fence
- Privacy Fence Commonly Cedar pickets; usually six-feet tall
- Pool Fence
- Post-and-rail fencing
- Roundpole Fences, similar to post and rail fencing but more closely spaced rails, typical of Scandinavia and other areas rich in raw timber. Slate fencing in Mid-Wales
- Slate Fence, a type of palisade made of vertical slabs of slate wired together. Commonly used in parts of Wales.
- Snow Fence
- Spear-top Fence
- Split-rail Fences made of timber, often laid in a zig-zag pattern, particularly in newly-settled parts of the United States and Canada
- Stake-and-wire fencing
- Turf mounds in semiarid grasslands such as the western United States or Russian steppes`
- Temporary fencing
- Vinyl fencing
- Wattle fencing, of split branches woven between stakes, or of moveable wattle hurdles.
- Wood-panel fencing
- Woven wire fencing, many designs, from fine Chicken wire to heavy mesh "sheep Fence" or "ring Fence"
- Wrought iron fencing, made from tube steel, also known as ornamental iron.

Prison	A prison is a place in which people are physically confined and, usually, deprived of a range of personal freedoms. Other terms are penitentiary, correctional facility, and jail , although in the United States "jail" and "prison" refer to different subtypes of correctional facility. prisons are conventionally institutions which form part of the criminal justice system of a country, such that imprisonment or incarceration is a legal penalty that may be imposed by the state for the commission of a crime.

Chapter 12. TOPICS IN THE ECONOMICS OF CRIME AND PUNISHMENT

Chapter 12. TOPICS IN THE ECONOMICS OF CRIME AND PUNISHMENT

Demand	In economics, demand is the desire to own anything and the ability to pay for it. . The term demand signifies the ability or the willingness to buy a particular commodity at a given point of time.
Demographic	Demographics data refers to selected population characteristics as used in government, marketing or opinion research). Commonly-used Demographics include race, age, income, disabilities, mobility (in terms of travel time to work or number of vehicles available), educational attainment, home ownership, employment status, and even location.
Crack epidemic	The Crack epidemic refers to the surge of crack houses and crack cocaine use in major cities in the United States between 1984 and 1990. Fallout from the Crack epidemic included a huge surge in addiction, homelessness, murder, theft, robbery, gang warfare, and long-term imprisonment. The first effects of the epidemic started in the early 1980s, but the DEA officially classifies the time of the epidemic starting in 1984 and ending in 1990, in what can be considered to be the height of the epidemic. The epidemic affected all major American cities.
Factor	A factor or limiting resource is a factor that controls a process, such as organism growth or species population, size, or distribution. The availability of food, predation pressure, or availability of shelter are examples of factors that could be limiting for an organism. An example of a limiting factor is sunlight, which is crucial in rainforests.

Chapter 12. TOPICS IN THE ECONOMICS OF CRIME AND PUNISHMENT

CPSIA information can be obtained at www.ICGtesting.com
Printed in the USA
LVOW021217291211

261560LV00001B/151/P